Yesterday's Sandhills

Yesterday's Sandhills

Wolf Children in Germany at the End of World War II

Rita Baltutt Kyle

Prospect
Avenue
Books
Olympia, Washington

Prospect Avenue Books LLC
Olympia, Washington

www.prospectavenuebooks.com

The views expressed in this work are solely those of the author and do not necessarily reflect the views of the publisher, and the publisher hereby disclaims any responsibility for them.

Printed in the United States of America

Edited by Michael L. Clark
Cover and Text Design: Michael L. Clark
Cover image: Strategic Property Investing Group LLC

Library of Congress Control Number: 2014904741
ISBN 978-0-9916179-1-3

Dedication

*For my dear Father, a gentle parent, kind and fair, the
rock of my upbringing and my life.   There is no one
closer to my heart; I will love him deeply till the day I die.*

Table of Contents

Preface

This is the story of the family of Rita Baltutt, who, at the end of World War II in the part of Germany known as East Prussia, came to be nearly destroyed, and how the four little girls, Edith, Rita, Irmgard, and Waltraut Baltutt came to be among those who were called Wolf Children.

The term "Wolf Children" (German: *Wolfskinder*) was the name given to orphaned German children at the end of World War II in East Prussia.

This is a matter that has been very seldom reported on, even in Germany, how the onslaught of the Soviet Red Army in the closing months of the European war caused thousands of children to be separated from their parents, most never to be reunited again.

When the Soviets conquered East Prussia in 1945, thousands of German children were effectively orphaned by their parents being killed during bombing raids, losing them during harsh winters without any food or shelter, or by the taking of their parents for forced labor. In many cases, older children tried to keep their siblings together, and survival — searching for food and shelter — became their number-one priority.

There were many different scenarios involving these children. Many of those near the borders of Lithuania made food scrounging trips there and were adopted by the rural Lithuanian farmers, who often employed them. Most of these children traveled back and forth repeatedly to bring food for their sick mothers or siblings.

Those left in the parts of East Prussia that became integrated into Poland generally melted into the arriving new Polish inhabitants, and some of them were deported to the Soviet Occupation Zone of East Germany. Similar stories existed for those left in the ruins of Königsberg, which became part of the Soviet Union.

The name "wolf children" came about because of their wolf-like wandering through the forests and along railroad tracks, sometimes catching rides on or in railroad cars.

There were some in Lithuania who assisted the German children to survive, but had to hide their efforts from the Soviet occupation authorities. For this reason many German children's names were changed, and only after the collapse of the Soviet Union in 1990 could they reveal their true identities. But many of them who were extremely young ended up largely forgetting who they were.

The Baltutt children were among those who became separated from their parents by virtue of those parents being taken from them in the drive by the Soviets to take as many forced laborers as possible into the Soviet Union.

This is their story, as written by Rita, the second eldest of the four girls.

--- Mike Clark

Prolog

Here I am sitting in front of a panel of judges in a political prison in the Soviet sector of Berlin. I am undressed with hands folded, being interrogated. And why am I in this humiliating position? The charge was not returning an East German Passport. The prosecutor wanted to put me away for 6 years for this grave insult. What I was really in trouble for was marrying an American serviceman; the passport was just a technicality. The West Berlin authorities had exchanged my East passport for a brand-new West passport when I married him. It was a ridiculous charge in any case. If I had come to the East Berlin authorities to give them my East Berlin passport they would have arrested me for wanting to leave their Communist "paradise."

Because it always took some time for immigration paperwork to be processed so a foreign-born serviceman's wife could enter the United States, my husband had had to return to the USA without me. I had to wait. And while waiting, one day I decided to visit my oldest sister to say goodbye, since I thought I might never see her again once I was in the United States. This was because she still lived in the Soviet sector of Berlin, otherwise known as East Berlin. But her neighbors had apparently noticed me, and

3

they knew who I was and also probably knew I had married an American. Since snitching on your fellow man is a Communist ideal, they notified the East German Police about me.

Harrison Soldier's Pretty Bride Disappears Into Red Germany

Wife Is Jailed By Communists, Husband Hears

The beautiful bride of a Harrison ex-GI has disappeared into the Russian zone of Germany. Earl Adams Jr., of Harrison, Route 1, heard his 18-year-old wife, Rita Baltutt, has been arrested and jailed by the Reds. But he can't be sure of her fate.

"People were always disappearing from the West Zone," he said. "The Russians never quit trying to get them back."

Earl, 22, married Rita last January, shortly before he left for the United States to be discharged from the Army.

Earl's mother, Mrs. Earl Adams Sr., said her son understood from the Army that it

EARL ADAMS JR., WIFE, RITA
. . . the Russians block their reunion

Newspaper Coverage of My Imprisonment

Suddenly there was a knock at the door. My sister opened it, and there were the police. They asked her if a Rita Baltutt was in her home. As soon as I heard the question, I quickly ran to the bathroom, locked myself in and looked for a hiding place for the West German currency I had on my person. This was because it was not permitted to possess West currency on the East side – it all had to be

4

exchanged for East currency when going through the border checkpoints. There were always patrols on the border and if caught you were taken to jail. I knew I was in enough trouble as it was.

As I was hiding the money, in the meantime my sister was very nervous and didn't know what to say – and of course she was also afraid – so she replied honestly, "Yes, Rita Baltutt is here," even though due to my marriage my surname was no longer "Baltutt".

So they arrested me and here I am in front of these judges.

They asked me, "How could you marry a war-loving American?" My answer, that love has nothing to do with politics, didn't go over very well. They warned me that when American soldiers marry here in Germany, they usually end up abandoning their wives once they were back in the United States.

They seemed minded to really throw the book at me, but my story about my childhood, about having my parents torn from me at the end of the war, and living alone with my sisters in the ruins of a town without any adult to take care of us, this seemed to increase their sympathy. I began to think that I might escape without a lengthy prison sentence.

Finally, after some consultation, they decided on what to do with me. Because of my youth and inexperience, my childhood story and what had happened to our family, and my clean record, they would only give me 3 months in jail. But after my release, they told me, I would no longer be allowed to visit West Berlin.

So here I am in this jail on a three month sentence and forbidden to leave East Berlin after my release (despite the fact that at that time people were normally permitted to go back and forth without too much interference). With this time on my hands I could reflect upon the amazing and terrifying course that my life had taken since the start of World War II. I remembered it like it was yesterday.

Part One – A Childhood in East Prussia

Chapter 1

When I was five years old, I remember the grown-ups hovering around the radio listening to the news of the German War that was soon to end and change my whole life. Like a child, I was not concerned and left concern for the future to the grown-ups.

The school I attended was the Queen Luise School in Osterode, East Prussia. My first day of school was on a sunny September day, 1942. My mother walked me to the classroom. It was tradition to give every child a 2 foot tall cone-shaped container and fill it up with candy and other goodies. I remember well that I was afraid to be left with a stranger and felt uncertain what school might have in store for me.

In 1943, under Hitler's regime the school was strict and impersonal. As soon as the teacher would enter the classroom, the first thing we were taught was to stand up every morning, raise our right arm and curtsey to a loud greeting "Heil Hitler, Herr Grünwald." Herr Grünwald would command us to be seated and proceed to call every child by his last name to check attendance.

In the first grade, we used a slate board with a sponge attached by a string for erasing. The first lesson in school was to learn how to draw the alphabetical letters in cursive.

We never learned how to print.

In mid-morning, the janitor would enter the classroom with a stainless steel pail and would offer every child a raw vegetable. It was routine in all German schools, for Hitler believed that good nutrition was necessary in order to raise a strong and healthy new generation, with good teeth and strong bodies.

I remember in school I was very shy out on the playground. As we stood in a circle to play a game, I was hoping that no one would pick me to jump around in the center for everyone to look at me. I always felt that I should be at home and that I really didn't belong with all those children.

Going home was the best part. I would walk along thinking what I could do after I arrived home. Maybe I could go with Edith, my sister, over to her girlfriend's house and she would tell scary stories about a witch named Gamorra who could change into a string and enter our bedroom through the keyhole of the door. Often, when I detected a string lying on the floor I was horrified.

Maybe they would offer to let me walk to the beach with them. There we could have a day of leisure and play in the water until dark.

We lived in a little house at Hauptstrasse 7 in the little fisher town, Senden, which lay right next door to Osterode. Our little house consisted of three rooms. In the bedroom, which was large, the beds were all lined up like in a hospital. My parents double bed, and twin beds for my older sister, Edith, and I. The other bed was shared by my two younger sisters, Irmgard, age five, and Waltraut, three. In the living room, my parents kept a chest of drawers, a chifferobe, an over-stuffed couch, and in the middle of the room a family table and chairs, with a lamp hanging from the ceiling whereby my mother could do all the sewing.

Often, when my parents would conduct their business in town, my sister, Edith, and I could investigate all the possessions they kept. Our chifferobe was built with a crown; and there my father would store his prized possessions, like his fishing equipment. We would climb up and spend hours looking over his things.

On one unfortunate occasion I opened his tackle box, poured out the fishing hooks, and found that they could pierce and bloody my hands. Quickly, I gathered them up in my dress only to discover and to my horror that the hooks became entangled in my good dress I wore to school each day. I was then frightened and tried to put all those things back exactly how I found them and climbed down from the chifferobe. My problem was not nearly solved, for I had a mass of hooks entangled in my dress.

I knew that Edith could solve this problem because, after all, she was two years older than I and therefore more intelligent. Her solution was to take the scissors and cut out the mass of hooks, leaving a large hole as large as a baseball. By then I was in a panic. We both decided the only way to conceal our mischief was to do away with the dress. We decided to wait until morning and climb to the attic of the house to hide the dress there and it would be gone forever. I was anxiously waiting for my mother to question me about the dress, but it never happened. She must have blamed the loss on the way she did her laundry.

In our little farm town, which was in the midst of many blue streams and rivers, the housewife did her laundry once a month in a huge kitchen which was equipped with giant copper kettles where the housewife boiled her laundry after it had soaked for three days. After the laundry had been boiled it was rinsed and scrubbed on a washboard, then boiled again. It was then laid out on the grass so that the sun could bleach it. After it laid on the grass to sun-bleach and dry it was sprinkled again and had to dry and sun-bleach once more. The laundry was then stretched and folded, and taken to a public press. There it was laid under a heavy roller and pressed. When it came out on the other end of the press it would look as neat and smooth as if it were made out of cardboard. So perhaps my mother would blame herself for losing my dress.

My home stood near the base of a sand hill. To get to the sand mountain, which had always been my favorite place, I had to pass an old man's hut.

The hut stood at the path to the hill and to pass the hut I had to observe it for a while to see if the old man was visible, for he allowed no one to be on his path. If he heard footsteps he would dart out of his hut, shout, and swing his cane at whomever passed by his door, but he would not follow anyone. So I would always run past his hut. I guess he only liked his privacy and could not tolerate trespassers.

The sand on the hill was white, so we called it sugar sand. I spent many hours building castles out of the moist sand, and I was proud because I built and owned them. There were weeds that grew there, but to me they were beautiful world of flowers swinging in the breeze, pink thistles, yellow dandelions and some pale pink flowers we called bells. I loved to pick off the heads of the bells to suck out the nectar, which tasted sweet and good.

The other side of the mountain led to a stream. We called it the horse stream because farmers would bathe their horses and cool them off there. There I could just take off my dress and swim in my underpants. It was customary at that time for children in Germany to swim naked up to the age of ten, and no one ever took notice.

When it became time for supper I would go home, skipping all the cracks in the sidewalk because if I stepped on one, Gamorra would surely appear that night.

My mother would have supper on the stove and as luck would have it, she would fry potatoes with sliced onions and I could not eat a bite. This was because the onion slices looked like worms after they were cooked and fell apart. I would look at my supper and sometimes even gag. In our household we had to eat what was put before us children and nothing else, so there could be no substitution just for me.

Of all my sisters I was the smallest of stature and very thin, with a pale face and white blond hair. I would not gain weight and had become a picky eater. My mother was a hard-working, robust and strong-looking woman with a robust figure and she tried to apply force to get me to eat. She told me that I better eat my supper or the wind would someday blow me away. This didn't work.

There was a time when my mother took me to our family doctor. He checked me over, took a fluoroscope of my body and told my mother I was anemic. He prescribed me vitamins and other medicine in powder form. Since I had to see the doctor, I was under the impression that I was really ill. In those days, people cured their ills at home with remedies passed on by their forefathers. Thinking that I must be seriously ill, I felt unusually good.

My mother gave my sister Edith the chore to go to the apothecary and get the drugs that were prescribed for my health. I walked to the city with her. The pharmacist handed us two packages. We paid and left, and as we headed back home we unpacked the bag and looked to see what he had given us. We discovered that some of the medicine had been wrapped in foil paper just like chocolates are wrapped. The pills were shaped round like lifesaver candy and were brown in color. We were wondering what they would taste like, and to our amazement they tasted just like candy, with a little bitter aftertaste. We sat at the edge of the sidewalk and shared the two rolls between us. We ate all of them and walked home to deliver the rest to my mother. She never realized that there was anything missing and as I learned later, the only thing the doctor had prescribed were vitamins. They had no ill effect on us.

The other package containing vitamins were supposed to be given to me at all my meals. It was in powder form and would float to the top of everything I ate. The taste was horrible and I refused to eat anything that it had been added to. Now, in order to get me to eat my mother had to refrain from sprinkling my food with the vitamins. After that, she tried to force me to swallow cod liver oil. That made me ill again. She finally gave up and seemed to accept the fact that I had to get strong and gain weight on my own.

Chapter 2

My father wasn't home much in those days. He was then forty years old and had served his time in the German Army, so didn't have to go to war. He was a machinist by profession and his skills were very badly needed in the munitions industry.

He worked for a company making tank and artillery ammunition in the city of Königsberg, about 300 kilometers north of Osterode. With this employment my parents, for the first time in their lives, could save half of the money my father earned. They talked about how in a few years they would have enough money saved to be able to afford a small patch of ground where they could build a home and have a small garden. My mother was a very good economizer and only spent money on necessities, so she had been able to save 10,000 German marks[1]. But in order to make their dream come true, they would have to save much more.

Father came home from the defense plant only two days a week. He arrived Friday afternoon and had to depart Sunday afternoon. Every Friday, before my father arrived home, my mother worked to have everything in good order. She cleaned the house, covered the table with a

---

[1]   This would be the rough equivalent of $66,000 in 2013 dollars.

white tablecloth and sometimes she even placed flowers on the table to make the house look homey and friendly. She went to the market to buy things my Father loved to eat when he was home. She wanted to treat him royally for they could only be together for less than two days each week. After she had prepared the house for him it was time to heat the kettles of water on the stove for our bath. She would sit each of us in a washtub and scrub us from head to toe.

I remember a few times my father would walk through the door while we were still taking our baths. He would hug my mother and with a big smile he would dry each of us with a towel, then set us on the bed with a hug and a kiss for a greeting.

My father was a tall and slender man, his hair brown and thin with high corners receding from his forehead. His face looked handsome to me. His gentle blue eyes would radiate loving kindness. My father was the center of my life, and I loved him. He was always fair with us children.

Every day of my entire life I will keep the memory of my father alive. There is never a time that I forget to include him in my prayers. I always see his face before me, the way he looked thirty years ago, and I think of the things he would do with us.

One warm summer day, when he came home from Königsberg he said to my mother while she was preparing dinner that he wanted to take my oldest sister, Edith, and I out in the boat. My sister and I were wild with excitement. We ran out to our shed to get the boat down, which was stored then between the rafters. After we managed to get it to the horse river, my father rowed it out to wide open water. Edith and I sat quietly on the wooden planks at the end of the boat.

My father liked physical exercise, such as gymnastics. He was also a very good swimmer and in his youth he had worked as a lifeguard. He asked Edith and I if we thought we had mastered swimming well enough to swim in the river. I could scarcely believe what he had said. I looked deep into the water and it looked almost black, which means that it is very, very deep. Edith, being two years older than I, always wanted to show our father that she could do almost anything and was not afraid of anything, said that she could swim just as well in the river as she could swim at the beach. Two weeks before that, my father tried to teach both of us at the beach how to relax in the water letting it carry ourselves without struggling. He taught me by holding his hand under my stomach, how to best use my arms and legs in a frog-like motion. I remember being frightened then, and now he wanted us to show him if we could swim in the deep water?

I knew that I did not want to swim in the deep water and wished that I had stayed home. My father then explained that we should always remember to let the water carry us and that it is much easier to swim in the deep water. We would soon be surprised what a joy it was. With that, my father took Edith and gently threw her overboard. I could see that there was no backing out and I was next. I could see my sister nervously trying to stay on top. My father took my arm and one leg and also tossed me in. The last thing in my mind was "let the water carry me". To my amazement, I discovered that he was right. It was very easy to make frog-like motions and just let the body of water carry me. I was so pleasantly surprised, that I could now swim in a river and I knew if I had to I could even swim in the ocean.

As we were finished and my father turned the boat to row toward home, the sun was setting in the west. The air was warm and the sky was decorated with "sheep" clouds. Every now and then from one of the oars a sprinkle of water would fall on my skin and it felt cold. The water seemed to be so mighty, I thought. I held my fingers in the water and let them trail behind the boat in the crystal clear water. I

17

felt that on that day I had taken a big step in overcoming fright and that I had accomplished something I had yearned to do – to swim out into the deep.

My father believed that gymnastics was essential for a strong and well-developed body. He paid special attention to posture; from the time I was small he would always tell Edith and me to walk with our chests out and our backs straight.

Edith would climb upon our table in the living room and make a hand stand and land feet first on the floor. My father would support her by holding his arm under her arched back. Over and over they would practice every weekend after he was home from Königsberg. She would show him how well she could master her acrobatics. My father asked me if I wanted to join the group; but I told him that I was afraid, and he did not insist.

My father would not go to the sand mountain with us. Instead, he liked to walk to the horse river. There he dived off contraptions that people had built for diving. Always in control, with his back arched and his arms spread out, he would do the swan dive. He would do gymnastics on the grass, like a track racer at the starting block he would push his legs up slowly. When his arms came to a full stretch, his legs would be straight up in the air. In this upside down position, he could then walk on his hands or stand as long as he pleased.

One of my father's homecoming trips turned out to be the best day in my life and will remain an everlasting memory. It was September.

My mother left the house to meet my father at the train station. Most people in those days did not have cars, so she would always walk. Soon she returned together with my father, who as usual laid his big black suitcase on the table, saying "I brought something for everybody." In excitement we all gathered around to see what he would unpack. This time he had brought each of us an orange and a chocolate bar! That was something really special for us kids. Normally, oranges were available only at Christmas time. And tropical fruit like bananas were almost never seen – I never tasted a banana until I was a teenager. And chocolate and candy as a rule were only given to kids at Easter or Christmas.

We were so overjoyed! Each one anxiously peeled her orange and then pulled off sections to eat. The taste of an orange was so different from the fruit that grew in East Prussia, and somehow the orange make it seem like Christmas. Chocolate, too, was something special. These two out-of-season treats were so special that we were careful not to use them up all at once. I saved my chocolate bar, which must have weighed a whole three ounces, for many days, only eating one square each day, to make it last longer.

But first, before eating any of it, I carefully studied the picture the chocolate was wrapped in. The picture showed a black boy sitting in the jungle with a lion next to him. Since I never in my entire life had seen a black person, I was fascinated. I wondered why his skin was black? I thought maybe since the sun in Africa was so hot that his skin must be blackened by the sun, and in my childish mind I knew that he must have white skin under his clothes.

I broke off a square of chocolate and let it melt in my mouth letting my senses taste it over and over. I wished that I could taste a piece each day forever. I looked at the foil that it was wrapped in, and saw that it was thin and fancy. Then I wrapped it back up, making it look like it hadn't been touched, and put it in my bed. The next morning, September 19th, was my seventh birthday and I awakened to find nothing out of the ordinary. It was a sunny day with the leaves just starting to transform to a pale green sprinkled with gold speck, like freckles.

Suddenly, my mother came into the bedroom, wished

me happy birthday and took me gently by the hand to lead me into the living room. There was my father standing next to something sparkling red and silver: a roller scooter! With a swoop he lifted me up by my waist, held me high against the ceiling and with a kiss he let me down saying, "Happy Birthday, Rita!" I turned toward my beautiful present. I could not believe that it was mine!

The frame of the scooter was made out of sturdy steel, with handlebars having a black rubber grip. The wheels were the size of a baby buggy's, with air balloon tires and sturdy silver spokes. Connecting the wheels was a platform with a paddle fitted with gears and a chain, just like a bicycle's, but most wonderful of all, in front there was a big letter "R" made out of chrome steel. It signified that I, and I alone, owned it. I was breathless with astonishment.

My father then told me that he had made it himself in the machine shop and it had taken many weeks to complete. He explained that the wheels of my scooter were running on ball bearings and that this scooter was capable of going very fast on straight surfaces and would go extremely fast downhill. I could not believe anything like that could be mine, and I had never seen anything that beautiful and powerful. My parents had a bicycle each, which they used to ride, and I had been looking forward to being old enough to ride them, but now I had a vehicle all my own!

They walked out to the sidewalk with me, and it was there that my father explained that the first pumps on the platform would be hard and slow. But as soon as I acquired some speed, I would be able to travel faster and faster. My father also warned me to be careful of people walking on the sidewalk, and to be careful when traveling downhill. My heart pounded with excitement and seemed to be choking me.

I took my roller scooter and drove away hoping my parents would not be watching me for I did not feel worthy of it. As I pushed the pedal back and forth, I started to go faster and faster. It felt smooth and easy, the gears were purring, and the balloon tires felt like I was riding on a cloud. The air was cool on my face and my hair blew in the wind. I pumped my scooter up to the next hill and turned left. I rode straight down faster and faster. The hill was deserted and I felt like I was the only living person in the world, going wherever I pleased on my roller scooter.

As I reached the bottom, I got off, leaned the scooter against a garden fence, and looked it over. "What a beautiful thing," I thought. I walked in front of it and looked at the shiny "R" placed in the very middle of the double frame. It sparkled in the sunlight like a mirror and seemed to blind my eyes. I wished I could ride on it and see the whole city as I had never seen it before, but I felt that I owed my parents the courtesy of returning and reporting on how I loved my scooter.

When I returned, my parents had gone into the house. I pushed my scooter into the hallway of the house. Then I asked if I could have it in the kitchen. My father asked how I liked it and if everything worked on it. I threw my arms around his neck and thanked him again. He stroked my hair and told me that it had been pure joy building it and that he had worked on it especially to be finished for my birthday. That night I went to sleep dreaming of tomorrow and the joy I would have with my scooter.

Chapter 3

The winter in my sweet home of Osterode, East Prussia, was cold. In our living room, we had a coal stove which was lit usually at mid-morning and fired about three times a day. The stove stood about 7 feet high and was tiled on the outside with 12 tiles. The tiles varied in each home; they could be various colors, such as green, brown, bone or white. Ours was a warm brown, and it was topped with a decorative crown at the top, leaving a 2 foot space to the ceiling.

When the stove was fired with coal, it radiated warmth all over the large living room. The living room was the only place where people kept these heating units. Most stoves had a stove bench built around it to sit and warm up when coming out of the cold in the winter.

My mother would sit on the stove bench and knit. I remember she'd knit long stockings and gloves for us children, and for herself she knitted a complete two piece suit. The suit was made up of a burgundy red skirt and a sweater jacket of burgundy with a black border at the sleeves and the bottom front.

When our stockings had holes, she taught us how to take yarn of the same color and darn the holes. It was hard to learn because it was like hand weaving. At first, all the yarn would cover the hole horizontally and then the yarn would have to be woven in vertically to completely close the hole. Edith could master it a little better than I and was praised by my mother. She made it look neat by cutting the jagged areas completely round, making a 360 degree circle. After we had completed our darning, my mother would inspect it carefully, and if it was not done to her satisfaction she would take the scissors and cut the hole open again. After weeks of darning our stockings, we could master it very well.

When going to bed at night my father taught Edith and I to carefully fold our clothes over a chair so they would be smooth and without a wrinkle in the morning. Every night we would carefully fold our clothing on a chair, all edges had to meet, so it would look like pages of a book. My father must have acquired this orderly task in the German Army and passed it on to us children.

The worst time for me at our house was when my mother started to do general house cleaning. It was like a disaster had struck our house. Every room in the house was in disorderly disarray. She would have clothing laying in piles all over the house. The furniture was stacked on top of each other. Everything imaginable was piled on tables. It looked like we were moving out of town.

At these times she worked herself into a frenzy and no one dared to get in her way. She was feverish, cleaning every drawer, cabinet, every piece of furniture and in the end she would scrub our unpainted wooden floors with a brush until they looked white. After the floors had dried she proceeded to put everything back in its place and the house smelled fresh and clean.

It was a big chore for her, and she could not be bothered with the slightest request by us. She would lose her temper, and in a very loud voice scold us, telling us to leave and not disturb her.

Chapter 4

My mother was one of seventeen children. She was brought up in a very strict Evangelical home with a very stern father and a soft hearted and kind mother. Her father was a hardheaded Prussian man who ruled with an iron voice. His word was the law and he never budged from his decisions. My mother disliked her father because of his stern and hardheaded nature, but she inherited his character and was somewhat like him.

In my mother's parent's home, religion was preached daily, and there was a strict code of conduct. My mother was never permitted to leave the house to attend a movie, or join social activities like dancing. When she grew into womanhood, she was still wearing long thick brunette braids down to her waist.

She was 20 years old when she met my father. They liked each other, but it was difficult for them to see each other. Nevertheless they secretly dated for some time, although grandfather had a feeling that something was going on. He became disgruntled about her disregard of the rules that he had set. Eventually she got into trouble and he told her that she had to leave the house.

She told Otto about it, and he immediately came to the house to ask my grandfather and grandmother for my mother's hand in marriage. They liked Otto a great deal, and everything turned out to the satisfaction of everyone – or almost everyone.

Otto's father was not at all pleased. In class-conscious East Prussia their family were part of the upper middle class, and considered my mother's family to be beneath them. When my father would not renege on his plans to marry my mother, he was disowned and disinherited.

It is important to realize that Otto was not interested in the young women of his social set. He could tell that they were only interested in high fashion and appearances, and many of them had no idea how to cook or how to take care of a household with all the chores necessary to do so. For him, my mother was exactly what he wanted, a practical woman who was not afraid of hard work.

So for this reason we children never met our grandfather on our father's side (our father's mother had died six years before our parents got married). Our father's father died just before the start of World War II.

My mother, then young, was a beautiful woman. She had the most beautiful, deep blue eyes. Her skin was olive and she had thick wavy dark brown hair. Her figure was well developed for her 20 years and she was of medium height. My father, then 30, was handsome and tall. He was a machinist by profession with a four-year apprenticeship and a good paying job.

Plans were made for the wedding, which was to take place on October 27, 1934. In the custom of the time, the wedding plans were quite elaborate, and involved both neighbors as well as family members. Much of the food was prepared well in advance, especially including sweet cakes and tortes of all kinds. Beef and fowl were butchered and prepared for that special day, and everyone possible, no matter where they lived, was invited. The furniture was moved and arranged for the wedding party.

On the day, my mother wore a beautiful bridal gown with a long train trailing at the back. Her head veil was decorated with a band made out of the green leaves and petals of the flower lily of the valley. In her hands she carried a bridal bouquet made of various colorful flowers. My father wore a black tuxedo with a white shirt and a white bow tie. It was a beautiful occasion for all.

Not long after the wedding my parents moved away from Memel forever. Memel at that time was not actually under German administration, because the Versailles Treaty which ended World War I had put it first under French control, and a few years later the Lithuanian government took over. Memel returned to German control in 1939 after Hitler's government demanded it.

The reason my parents moved away from Memel was the dramatic expansion of the German Army in 1935, which made it very attractive in those last days of the Great Depression. My father served about three years in the Army, stationed at a military post at the town of Gilgenburg, East Prussia. This was where their first child, Edith, was born.

My mother had this to say about Edith, her first born: "She was a beautiful baby, bald when she was born, with blue eyes. She was a healthy child with rosy checks and a fierce temper."

By the time my father was released from the German Army I had arrived and my mother was pregnant with her third child, also a daughter, who was to be named Irmgard. Demands for armament production had opened up, and my father's skills as a machinist were in great demand. He was able to secure a position at a company manufacturing artillery ammunition. The factory was located in Königsberg, the capital city of East Prussia. It was probably a position with Waggonfabrik L. Steinfurt AG, a long-established manufacturing firm in the East Prussian capital of Königsberg, on the Baltic Sea. Although Steinfurt's primary business since its founding in 1830 was the manufacture of horse-drawn wagons, carriages, streetcars and eventually railroad rolling stock, after Hitler assumed power in Germany and the military buildup began, Steinfurt added ammunition manufacturing to its business.

But rather than moving the entire family to Königsberg, we settled in Osterode, and my father lived and worked in Königsberg during the week. He was home on the weekends and the pay was very generous. He not only earned his salary, which was more than he needed, but he also had extra benefits, such as separation pay for his family.

In September 1939 Hitler invaded Poland, starting World War II, and our troops burned cities, and tortured and killed innocent people. After Hitler's army conquered the western part of Poland (with the Soviets occupying the eastern) captured Polish soldiers and many civilian men were rounded up, and shipped to Germany to help take the place of German workers who were serving in the military. After June 1941, when Germany invaded the Soviet Union, prisoners from those lands were added to the mix.

My father's employer was among those in Königsberg who received forced laborers, in this case mostly from White Russia, or Belorussia[2], giving them the unpleasant task of making ammunition to fight their own brothers. My father was assigned the responsibility of supervising those working in his department. He was sympathetic to the prisoners and saw to it that they were treated as well as was in his power. Although it was forbidden to establish friendships with the prisoners, my father nevertheless taught them to

---

2 Belorussia was east of Lithuania and Latvia, and bordered on the south by Ukraine and on the southwest by Poland.

speak German and in return they taught him to speak Russian. This became important to us later.

Being natives of Memel, which was almost surrounded by Lithuania, both my father and mother could speak some Lithuanian, although mother spoke it better.

By the time of Germany's invasion of the Soviet Union, my parents had added two more daughters to our family: Irmgard, born December, 1938; and Waltraut, born December, 1940.

One incidental benefit of my father's supervision of forced laborers was spare time that he could use to occupy himself with making presents for my mother and us children.

For us little ones, he made plush toys, and a butterfly on wheels. With a precision saw, he cut out the wings and the body. He painted the butterfly black and sky blue. The antennae were made out of spirals with small steel balls on the ends. If you pushed the toy, the butterfly would open and close her wings as if flying.

Waltraut, the youngest of my sisters, had a monkey made the same way. When pushed, the monkey would juggle three balls which were attached to a metal rod.

For my mother he built an electric hotplate with two burners. At that time in our community such an appliance was considered ultramodern – most people had no other choice but to set a fire in a stove with coal briquettes in order to cook. When he brought this hotplate out from his luggage, mother's face radiated suspense. She wasted no time in trying it out and immediately plugged it into the electric socket. I too watched this marvel, and was fascinated to see the wire spirals heat and slowly turn red hot when switched on.

Mother was very pleased. I could see it in her face. She knew how much of a luxury it was – something not everyone had.

Chapter 5

One summer day my teacher, Herr Grünwald, urged all the children in my class to go out into the woods and collect as many acorns as we possibly could. The acorns were taken to a laboratory to make medicine for all the wounded soldiers in hospitals all over Germany. He declared that all German people, young and old, had to help their country to win the war. I felt enthusiastic and took it personally that I could take part in helping to win the war and live in peace.

Edith and I took a metal bucket and walked to a park behind a church where we knew there were many oak trees. It was peaceful there, the birds chirping their sweet melodies and the squirrels scurried in the underbrush, collecting their share of acorns for the winter. We tried to gather all we could but the bucket did not fill quickly. No matter how hard we picked acorns off the ground it seemed we could not fill the bucket over the half mark.

I was getting tired and sat under an oak tree, looking into my treasure. The acorns looked so very much like hazelnuts that I so loved. I thought that something that delicious looking must taste good, too. I peeled an acorn, took the fruit, broke it in half and looked at the fruit itself. It looked good enough to eat. I took a bite and to my horror

I discovered that it tasted very bitter, like poison I spit it out and wiped my tongue with my sleeve.

Edith and I were getting tired of looking for acorns and decided to take our buckets and go home. We walked along the street, thinking how patriotic we were, helping the wounded soldiers all over in hospitals. As we walked along, suddenly a column of prisoners appeared, guarded by armed German soldiers who marched alongside of them, with their guns pointed at the prisoners.

I carefully looked at the sight passing me by. The prisoners wore brown uniforms. They all looked shabby and distressed, their uniforms worn and unkempt, faces without expression, and their eyes looked straight ahead or down at the asphalt road. Some of them wore old shoes and others had canvas wrapped around their feet. I believe that those were the ones who had no shoes. Each prisoner had a big letter "P" painted on the back of his uniform, identifying them as Poles.

I felt utter sadness for those men. My heart cried out to help them, but I was powerless. I thought, if I was a high princess, like in Grimm's Fairy Tales, I would order the German guards to release those men and let them go home to their families.

Going to sleep that night, I could still see the sad faces of the Polish prisoners.

The next day, when I visited my favorite playground, the sand hills, I was sitting by my favorite project, my castle, building back up what the wind had blown down, my fence. I was letting the white sand run through my fingers, when I heard the sound of an airplane flying over the sand hills. Looking up saw that it was a German Army plane, recognizing it from the swastika marked on its tail. It was also a double decker – it had double wings, a biplane. It was a lucky omen to see a double decker and to see one meant a wish could be made. Quickly, I thought of a wish.

I wished that when I grew up that I would marry a prince and could become a princess.

At the sand hills, my imagination could wander. There I could be anybody and the sand hills could be anyplace: a desert, a Garden of Eden, a city, or a farm. I could be a queen there, a mother, a beautiful movie star, or a rich girl.

Today it was a castle, and in the center of my castle stood a table that I made likewise from sand, and I picked colorful flowers and stuck them into the moist sand of my table. And then I walked down the hill to the horse river to take a swim, and then walked home.

Arriving home I found that there was a surprise. A package had arrived from the city of Leipzig. My father's brother and his wife lived in Leipzig with their two children, Irma and Horst. Irma was a teenager and studied music at the Conservatory. She learned to play the piano and took singing lessons. She had outgrown her toys and had sent to us her favorite doll. The doll was wrapped in newspapers and wood shavings to protect its beautiful head, which was made out of porcelain china. The doll was about 2 feet tall, with a torso made out of plastic. Its face was really beautiful, with blue eyes that opened and closed for sleeping, and light blond hair. This doll was the first and only doll we had ever owned. My mother explained that the doll belonged to all us children and to take good care of it, for the head was breakable.

My Aunt Elsa had sent all the clothes that belonged to the doll and we named her Irma after our cousin who once owned it.

One day my dear father came home from Königsberg and brought with him a doll buggy. He himself had made it, an indescribably beautiful buggy. Its wheels were small, with metal spokes, and it had a small but roomy body. The top part was suspended with springs which gave it a spring-like bounce. The push handle was made from chrome and the body was painted white and green. It had a hood made of white canvas which could fold down like an accordion or be up to enclose the doll.

Edith and I laid the doll in the buggy and took it out for a walk on the sidewalk. As we walked along, taking turns to push it, a lady walked up to us. She admired the doll buggy and asked where we had bought it. Edith told the lady that it was not bought but made by our father. These are all the things that will keep my father alive in my memory.

Edith and I played many beautiful hours with our beloved doll Irma. One day as we dressed the doll and took her for a walk in the buggy, we took turns holding and fondling it, like it was our baby. Suddenly, the doll slipped out of my hands and slammed to the sidewalk. In horror, I watched its head split into large pieces and the eyes fell back into its head.

As we carefully picked up the pieces, we looked at each other. It would be hard to go home now and tell our mother the tragic news. We laid the broken doll back into the buggy, and with tears running down our cheeks we walked home to tell our mother what had happened. Surprisingly, my mother was calm and seemed to understand that it had been an accident that we all felt very bad over.

In weeks to come, my mother asked all her friends what could be done about the doll's broken head. No one had a good answer. A lady friend of my mother's suggested we send it to a doll clinic in Berlin and have it repaired there.

Berlin seemed so far away and it was like sending Irma to the end of the world. My father suggested gluing the pieces together and filling the splintered holes with face powder, mixing it to get the proper color. So that is what we tried.

The head was glued back together, the eyes put back into position and powder samples were made up with the right shade of rosy pink. We filled in the cracks with missing splinters with the powder and glue mixture, and then carefully sanded down the excess so it was smooth.

The doll was now repaired with the head back on its torso, but the broken places were clearly visible and the doll was just not the same doll any longer. It felt like playing with an object, not a beautiful doll with dark blue eyes and a rosy baby face. This had been the only doll I ever owned and also had to be shared. I never owned another doll.

Chapter 6

Easter in my homeland was very memorable. It was somewhat like Halloween in America, because children would go from house to house, ringing doorbells and saying a rhyme. People would then put jellybeans or hard boiled colored Easter eggs into our baskets. We would then go home and sort out all the candy and eat everything we had collected. I remember so well my father spending Easter morning with us. He would wake us and tell us "Get dressed! We have to go out Easter egg hunting!" We would then dress hurriedly and be quickly ready to go.

One of these times we walked for a long stretch until we arrived at the edge of a wood and turned in. It was morning and the sun was giving the woods a golden shine of spring warmth.

My father asked us to start looking in an area he pointed out, saying that it looked like the Easter bunny had his home there. We started to search under trees and shrubs and there...a beautiful nest with colorful Easter candy.

Anxiously, we continued to look under shrubs and there was another nest with hard boiled eggs of every color in the rainbow. Our baskets were now filled with chocolate eggs, jelly beans, and boiled eggs.

As we walked out of the woods into an open patch of grass, suddenly out of nowhere appeared six wild rabbits. Spotting us, they shot across the field and disappeared into the woods. If I never believed in the Easter bunny before then, I believed in him now. It seemed to make Easter so complete and was like magic.

As we walked homeward my father, being sport minded, told us to wait and when he raised his arm we were to try our darnedest to race to him. The one that got to him first would receive as a reward a candy egg. As we raced several times, my father made sure that each of us received a fair amount of rewards.

The rest of the way I held his finger in my hand. (My hand was too little to hold his big hand.) We arrived home and found that my mother had set the table in a festive manner.

It was customary in my homeland of Germany to eat goose at Christmas and duck or chicken at Easter. Also, the housewife started to prepare cakes and fancy tortes a week in advance. The table was set with the best white linen cloth and only the best dishes were used for the occasion. The kitchen smelled of fowl baking in the oven and the fowl was stuffed with apples, raisins, and onions, and sometimes figs. The wings of the fowl and the neck were used to make a clear broth containing noodles which was eaten as an appetizer. The main course was the meat, potatoes and always red cabbage as a vegetable, made to taste sweet and sour. For the occasion my mother always wore a white apron that covered her entire dress. It was tied in the back with a big bow.

After the holidays there was always a lot of food left to eat, like cakes and cookies.

In 1942, some time after Easter, my mother received a letter from my grandmother telling her it was urgent that she come back to Memel at once. My grandfather was ill, suffering from pneumonia, and grandmother needed her to be there. My mother hurriedly packed a few of her things, made arrangements to have a teenage girl keep an eye on us two older girls, took my two little sisters Irmgard and Waltraut with her and left on an afternoon train.

Edith and I had to go to school during the daytime and ate dinner at a neighbor's house. Their daughter would then take us home to sleep. Edith and I had never been alone before and tried to keep busy by playing games. Edith asked if I wanted to play checkers. Sitting up in our bed we would keep each other amused by playing checkers for hours.

At one point, one of the checker disks fell between the mattress and the wooden bed frame. Edith and I tried everything we could think of to retrieve the disk but it seemed to be lost forever. Edith then had an idea to lift up the mattress and the box spring and with a knife slide the disk to the floor. As we lifted the mattress and the box spring, it became too heavy to hold onto and we let it fall. As it fell, it got wedged between the bedframe, laying cockeyed.

We tried in vain to lift it back up into the bedframe but to no avail. Edith, being two years older than I, much bigger boned and stronger looking, was now under the bed lifting the box spring with her back. It didn't budge. Finally, in some desperation, we made the bed, trying to make it look normal, fluffing the feathers of the blanket more toward one side than the other, but it still looked very crooked.

We were now worried what our mother would say on her arrival home, seeing the house in disarray. It wasn't yet too bad – but we still had two more days before she was due to arrive. Plenty of time to make things worse!

The next morning I was up early getting dressed for

37

school. I had a couple of hours before I had to go to school and I proceeded to search in the kitchen china hutch to see if my mother might have stored away some goodies in a secret place.

I must have been about 4 feet tall at the time, and had to climb on a kitchen chair to get to the bottom part of the hutch. There I stood, looking in all the jars, opening lids, and finally I found what I thought I was looking for – round tablets. They were very dark, almost black and I thought, "It must be chocolate."

I stuck one in my mouth and sucked on it a little when suddenly I felt a horrible brassy taste in my mouth. Spitting it out into my hand I found it was as black as soot. I let it fall onto the white china hutch, but found as I was wiping the black stuff from the furniture that it smeared more and more the color of deep blue. What I thought were delicious candies were tablets that were used to make ink. Just one of the tablets could make a coffee cup full of rich blue ink.

Now I ran to the water faucet to wash my hands and wet some towels to clean the mess. As I tried to wash it off, the ink simply spread more and more. My hands were now blue and it would not wash off. I tried in vain to clean off the hutch and only this only spread it even more. By now the hutch looked ruined. I had every towel out of the linen drawer in a big mess pile.

I looked at the time. It was time to leave for school. But when I looked in the mirror, I could not believe what had happened to me. My tongue was as black as coal and my teeth looked almost the same, only they had a blue tint. I was frightened about leaving, but I felt like I had to get out of that house of horror. I walked to the chifferobe and took my brand new coat from a hanger, the coat I was not to wear to school but only on Sundays or holidays. I loved that coat because it had pockets. I thought that by wearing my best coat I could put my hands in the pockets so that they wouldn't show the horrible blackish blue ink that stained my hands. I could manage to keep my mouth shut and no one would take notice of the color inside my mouth.

Sitting in the classroom with my spring coat on, I managed all right until recess. At recess, all the children were playing games in the schoolyard. I was standing at a fence with my hands in my pockets watching the others. Suddenly two girls came running over to me, pulled my arm, and asked me to come along and play their game. By then one of my hands was jerked out of my pocket and the other girl noticed my hand.

With a loud yell she screamed, "Oh, look at your hands! What did you do to them?" When I explained that I had spilled ink all over them, they also noticed my discolored teeth. With a shriek they ran off getting the other classmates to come over and look at me. I felt like a freak. I could not bear for the other children to come and stare at me and I decided to run for home.

The next day my mother was due to arrive home from Memel. It was late afternoon when Edith and I walked to the train station to meet her. We spotted her getting off the train holding baby Waltraut and leading Irmgard by the hand.

My mother looked very pretty as she got off the train. She was wearing her best clothes, and a dark gray overcoat with a large gray Persian lamb collar and a light gray felt hat. We ran over to greet her and to help with her suitcase. She smiled happily and gave us a kiss and a hug for hello.

As we walked to our home, my mother asked how we had gotten along at home. We hesitated a little and then told her that everything except for the bed was in good order.

While walking I felt a strange sensation all over my body. I felt prickly and itchy. When I tried to scratch my body it felt somewhat numb.

Arriving home my mother first walked into the

bedroom to put down her things. She immediately noticed the lopsided bed and scolded Edith for that. Walking into the kitchen she was confronted with the ruin I had created there. There was more of the blue on the floor and the hutch looked disgraceful. She told both of us that our father was soon to arrive from work and that we would discuss everything then. She heated the water for our bath and I was second in line to get scrubbed.

As soon as my mother took a look at me she knew what had happened. I was suffering from a reaction caused by swallowing some ink. My body had broken out in hives and looked red and swollen. I knew my mother was concerned because she reacted quietly towards me. Under other circumstances, after seeing what I had done I would have been punished. After the bath she dried me off and said that we would have to go see the doctor tomorrow.

When my father walked into the house, Edith was sitting on the bed and I was standing on the oven bench to be inspected by him. My father showed no sympathy for me and told my mother that I deserved to be punished for what I had done. At that time, however, no one was punished. As soon as he walked into the bedroom, he took the bed frame apart and made it look normal again.

When I visited the doctor the next morning, he examined me thoroughly, put me behind a fluoroscope and found everything to be all right. This time he did not prescribe any medicine and the next day I began to feel normal again[3].

---

[3] The tablet mostly likely consisted of the chemical known as Prussian Blue, a beautiful blue pigment used in oil and water colors, which was and still is widely used in inks. Fortunately for Rita, Prussian Blue is non-toxic.

Chapter 7

And then it was summertime. The seasons in my hometown of Osterode, East Prussia, were very much like the seasons in Ohio where I live now. In winter, we had snow and spent many days sled riding or we would ice skate on a frozen lake, but it was the summer season I loved most of all. I could roam the sand hills or swim at the beach. Edith and I could sit with our girlfriend, Helma Sontofski, and tell scary stories about the witch Gamorra.

Each August my parents made plans to ride into the thick forests to pick as many blueberries and mushrooms as they could find. They each had a bicycle which had been equipped with two children's seats on each bike. In the front, attached to the handle bar, was a small but safe baby seat made out of bamboo. On the back, on top of the fender, was a black metal seat which had been equipped with a backrest. So we could have all gone out for mushrooms and blueberries.

But for this kind of expedition, Irmgard and Waltraut stayed at home with our neighbors. It was easier not to have to worry about them, for then we could pick more blueberries and mushrooms than if we had to worry about them.

On these occasions Edith and I would each occupy the

front seat made out of bamboo. I then felt like I was leading the way. Riding along endless miles on a black asphalt road, seldom did we see other bicycles or even a horse cart. Sometimes we would be passed by a pickup truck. The ride must have lasted two hours as we would pass through nothing but farmland or open green meadows with cattle or horses grazing in the sun. After we arrived at the forest we continued to ride on until we reached the first or second fork. We then rode on that path deep into the forest. The trees there were thick and all their trunks were big in diameter.

When the wind rustled through the branches the sound was like ocean waves coming up to the beach. The forest was dense and dark. A ray of sun would glisten through the trees and from afar there was the call of the cuckoo bird, which could never be seen, but often was heard. Colorful salamanders would give us a frightful scare and quickly disappear under the moist, cool foliage or hide under the green moss.

As we walked farther we came to an opening. Surrounded by trees was a meadow and in the center, there was a small pond. I rested there. The pond was crystal clear and surrounded by flowers of all kinds. Crickets chirped their midday song and the bees were humming while hanging on the blossoms to collect their nectar. A butterfly as beautiful as the rainbow fluttered by and rested on a blue blossom which we call a corn flower. The sweet smell of the *erika*, known in English as heather, which are light purple and sometimes grow for miles, overcame my senses. My eyelids felt heavy. The sun's warm rays enveloped my body and the still wind cooled my face. I felt that I was falling into the sweet world of sleep.

Suddenly, I heard Edith calling out my name, "Rita!" She came running toward me waving her arms. "Where have you been?" she asked. "Don't you know that we are here to pick blueberries? Come at once!" she commanded.

Slowly, I brushed and smoothed my dress and followed Edith back into the forest. Both my parents looked busy, with their bodies bent over, holding the blueberry plant with one hand and picking off the berries with the other.

As I approached my mother, she looked up and told me that I must not run off into the woods by myself for I could get lost in the forest and maybe never be found again. She walked over to our utensils we brought with us and handed me a metal cup.

"When this cup is filled with berries" she explained, "you can empty it into the pail." The bottom of the pail was barely covered with berries. I thought to myself, "I wonder if we have to completely fill the pail?" That would take until nightfall, I thought. I walked behind my mother looking for a nice thick patch with lots of blueberries. I could see plenty of plants. The ground was thick with the dark green blueberry plant, but where were the berries – they were not all that plentiful. All I could see was that every plant held maybe three to seven berries. I thought to myself that it might take hours before I could fill my cup. If there were as many berries as leaves on the plant my cup could be filled in no time. I bent over to pick three that I could see.

I thought to myself as soon as I have the bottom of my cup covered it should not take long to fill the cup halfway. I walked over to where Edith was picking berries to see how full she had filled her cup. Her cup was over a quarter filled, but I had barely covered the bottom of mine. Edith looked at me and with a smile she said, "I tell you what – I'll eat my blueberries until our cups are even and then we'll have a race to see who can fill her cup up first." I agreed and was eager to beat her in the race.

It was then that I discovered the secret. When I bent the plants to the side I discovered that most of the berries were hidden from the eye because they grew on the underside of the plant. I found big ones and little ones. I

43

picked them first into my hand, and when my hand could not hold any more, I then emptied my hand into the cup, which was now half full. When I came upon some big ripe berries I would upset my cup and fill my mouth with them. They tasted very sweet, juicy and cool.

The more berries I tasted the less I filled my cup. They tasted so very delicious that I had to get my fill. Blueberries stain, and very soon my tongue, teeth an hands, even the skin around my lips had taken on the color blue. Edith also loved blueberries and by looking at her discolored mouth and teeth she had also filled her stomach instead of her cup.

As we walked back to where the blueberry bucket was kept, I noticed my mother standing there. Looking into the bucket I noticed it was filled half way with delicious berries. Edith and I poured into the bucket what we had picked, but it did not seem to fill it any fuller. My parents had intentionally set out to do what they had come to do and deserved the credit for their harvest. My mother now explained that there wasn't much time left, for we had to reach home before dark, and that we would spend a little time picking mushrooms. She then lead Edith and I to a mossy area, picked a mushroom and showed it to us. She then told us to look it over very carefully and not to pick any other kind, for there are more poisonous than there are edible.

By now, my parents were picking mushrooms, but they would pick several varieties, for they knew the good from the bad. Gathering mushrooms was not as tedious as picking berries. Soon we had a nice batch of maybe five pounds. I noticed my father had started to gather up our treasures and arranged to head for home. The pail with the blueberries was hung on the handlebar of my father's bicycle and the basket with the mushrooms dangled from the handlebars of my mother's bike.

My father called out for Edith and my mother that it

was now time to head for home. He lifted me up into the bamboo seat in front of the bicycle that was my mother's. She was carrying me because I was lighter in weight. Edith would ride on the handlebars in the seat of my father's bicycle.

The sun was now leaving the horizon, like a giant fireball its edge slipping behind a broad wall of hazy clouds. Soon it would be twilight. The wind was now cool and I felt tired and cold. Riding along on the long stretch of asphalt the forest on either side of the road looked spooky and sinister. I thought of Hansel and Gretel being lost in the woods. I felt secure on my mother's bike, knowing we would soon be home.

The next day my mother was busy preparing the blueberries and mushrooms for canning. To detect any poisonous mushrooms my mother used a traditional method handed down for many generations. She boiled them in a large kettle and inserted a silver spoon. Supposedly if the spoon took on a black color then a poisonous mushroom had been mistakenly picked for an edible one, but if the spoon stayed silvery clear then there was no danger.[4]

Out of the blueberries my mother made jelly and pudding, and gave us a bowl with plenty of berries with sugar and milk. These foods remain a favorite to me. There are certain things that will remain with me always as a touch of home.

---

[4] This is actually not true, but a myth that has been around for a long time with no basis in fact. To date no mushroom toxins are known to have this reaction with silver.

Chapter 8

The city of Memel, the home of my grandparents, is situated at the extreme north and east of East Prussia on the Baltic Sea. Originally founded by Germanic people in the 12th Century, it was German over most of its history, until the aftermath of World War 1, when by treaty Germany lost control over it, and then in 1924 allowed to be administered by Lithuania. It was very desirable because of its rich soil, its ice-free seaport, and its industries.

But in 1939, Hitler by ultimatum demanded its return and it became German territory again, but only until the war's end. After the Second World War in 1945, with all Germans driven out, it was given to Lithuania permanently. There my maternal grandparents had lived all their lives, from 1870 to 1944.

It was the summer of 1942, school was out, and one morning my mother dressed to have her hair coiffured at the beauty parlor and then went shopping afterward. When she arrived home she had many packages. There was meat, butter, and cold cuts from the butcher, hard yeast rolls, which had just been baked and were still warm to the touch and a treat for us kids, and "butterkeckse" or butter cookies.

Lying on the table in a fancy bag from the dress shop

there were two red dresses, almost identical except for the embroidery on the front yoke. One had been embroidered across the yoke with daisies surrounded by green leaf stitchery and the other dress had been embroidered with bluebell flowers, also imbedded with green leaf stitchery. There were also white satin ribbons for our hair.

My mother turned to me and announced that we would pack a suitcase that evening and all of us would travel to Memel the next day. She told me that I was going to remain with my grandparents for the summer and my grandmother would see to it that when I returned that I would have some meat on my bones.

The next morning, wearing me wearing my new dress and a big white ribbon in my hair, we walked to the train station. As the train pulled into the station, Edith held Irmgard by the hand, a conductor helped with the suitcase while my mother carried our younger sister, Waltraut, in her arms. We took seats on long shiny wooden benches. Edith and I had a window seat. Soon the conductor blew his whistle and the train began to move. If felt so good to be on a train, going out into the world! The distance between the city of Memel and my hometown was about 450 kilometers, and a full day's journey. A long time for children to sit in one place, but people talking to us on the trip made it pleasurable.

Upon our arrival at Memel's train station, we were greeted by one of my grandparents' neighbors and his horse-drawn cart. We boarded his cart and he transported us to their door. When we arrived at their little house, and grandmother and grandfather hurried outside to greet us, I saw that my grandmother was a tiny person, barely four feet eight inches tall. She wore an accordion pleated skirt which reached to the tip of her shoes and an apron that tied at her waist, that was as long as the skirt. She had dark brown hair, without a trace of grey, which was braided with the braids neatly wound about her head. She was then 72 years old and had no teeth at all. Her blue eyes were faded from age and I detected humility and hurt in them.

My grandfather was also not tall in stature, and was likewise slight of build, but his hair was grey and he sported a handlebar mustache. Being a properly stoic Prussian paterfamilias, he was careful not to show any outward emotion as he greeted us children with a pat on the shoulders, but in his grey eyes I detected a sparkle of joy to see us

The house was very small and simple. In a corner of the kitchen, stood a black iron coal stove. There was an old fashioned water faucet mounted on the wall and beneath it was a barrel type drain to drain the running water. By the window was a clean scrubbed wooden table with chairs. On a shelf, which was mounted on the wall, was a hurricane lamp.

The living room was simple but very homey. There was the traditional heating unit covered with decorative tile and surrounded by the usual oven bench. In the middle of the room stood an oval table covered with a linen cloth embroidered with colorful needle work. This table cover was something my grandmother had worked on during the dark winter days. There was a chest of drawers, a small table by the window on which stood a fancy hurricane lamp with a big milky glass shade. In the corner of the room, against the wall, was my grandmother's bed which was covered with a patchwork quilt she had sewn. On the wall by the bed hung a beautiful tapestry of black velvet with a picture of a white swan swimming in the moonlight on a silver blue lake. There was another small room that my grandfather shared with his 30 year-old invalid son. He was the only one of their children still living at home.

Hermann was paralyzed on the right side of his body. He was tall, had dark brown hair and blue eyes. On the right side of his forehead, he had a deep indentation in which the beating of his pulse could be clearly seen. To me it was very grotesque. He spoke with a slur and when he walked, he dragged one leg behind the other. His right arm was hung limp by his side.

I was immediately afraid of him. Whenever I was around him I would keep a careful eye on him, my attention always drawn to his pulse beating in his forehead. I knew I could never make friends with him, and felt like I should hide from him.

When Hermann was 22 years old, he had been invited by one of his friends to ride in a car. This would have been in 1934. In order to start the motor, it had to be cranked until it kicked over. On that day, Hermann volunteered to crank it, and, as he did so, the motor started and the iron crank hit him in the forehead, broke and penetrated his skull. He was in a coma for several weeks. When he awoke from his coma, he had suffered irreversible brain damage and was paralyzed on the right side of his body. The doctors gave his parents no hope and told them to prepare for the worst, that he would not survive. They were wrong. His strong nature repaired his wounds but left him hopelessly paralyzed. His mind was not affected and being so young he realized his predicament and became very hard to live with. There were times when he screamed at my grandmother and his blue veins protruded from his neck and forehead. These times brought tears to my grandmother's eyes. My grandmother told him of the Lord, that he must have faith, but Hermann would not listen. He screamed at her until his voice gave out and his pulse in the cavity of his forehead beat more rapidly than ever. He would then storm out of the house, trying to walk fast just to get away from his wrecked youth. I never knew where he would go after his outbursts, but he would always return late, shuffle into the tiny bedroom and go to sleep.

Chapter 9

Not long after we arrived in Memel my mother and my three sisters returned to Osterode, leaving me in the care of my grandmother. It was her intention to see that I gained weight and looked strong by the time I returned home, and she took extra care in feeding me.

Every morning without fail I found a large bowl of oatmeal cereal, steaming hot, on the table. In order to encourage me to eat it, my grandmother provided a sweet reward: a peppermint candy stick lying beside my dish. She told me that if I finished my oatmeal I could then have the peppermint stick; but if I did not finish my oatmeal, I must leave the candy, too.

And oh, how I hated oatmeal! I tried so hard to eat all of it. Looking at the peppermint stick I pretended that it was candy I was swallowing but it did not always work. I gagged and cried but most of the time I managed to finish my oatmeal. Then I would gladly take the peppermint stick and run outside to play.

My grandmother was the most perfect person I have ever known in all my life. It seemed to me that she lived as close to the Bible as it was humanly possible to do. She honored the Sabbath day by cleaning her little house and doing all her work on the weekdays, and resting on Sunday. Even the meal for Sunday had to be prepared the day before.

She suffered from severe rheumatoid arthritis and could not always walk to church. On those Sundays when her joints would not permit her going to church she worshipped our Lord at home. On Sunday, as every day, she arose at dawn. Kneeling on her aching knees by her bed she prayed before God. She then dressed herself in her best clothing, which consisted of an accordion pleated black skirt made of the best gabardine, a black silky apron, a black, long sleeved blouse, and a white babushka head scarf. She then sat by the window in the living room and read her Bible until it was time for dinner.

My grandfather and Hermann never participated with her in prayer and she never tried to force them, but they knew not to disturb her on Sunday.

Every night before retiring for bed my grandmother rubbed medicine onto her red swollen knees. She called it "snake venom." It had the smell of Ben-Gay.

One day, after my grandmother gave me a bath and washed my hair, I was standing before her in the living room by the big oval table. She sat on a chair, combing my hair and I was naked from the waist up. My grandmother looked me over and said, "You are a nice little girl, Rita. You look like a little angel. In fact," she said, pointing at my shoulder blades, "these are the beginning of your wings and someday they will grow into angel wings." I was very much taken by what she said. I believed that someday I would surely be an angel.

My grandmother and I shared her bed that stood in the living room alongside a wall. I slept next to the beautiful black velvet tapestry and could never see enough of the beautiful white swan swimming in the moonlight with the stars shining down on him.

My grandmother would always tell stories about God and his son, Jesus. She said that our almighty God is our

Heavenly Father and that we are his children. She said that he loved all of us and that he wants us to be humble, unselfish, and that we should never ask for riches or overabundance. We must only ask humbly for things that we desperately need. We should never show greed. She told me that the Bible is the word of God and that it speaks the truth only. The Bible foretells the Second World War and that most people don't understand the powerful word of God.

She told me that mankind is suffering from greed and that our Father is angry, that he will send fireballs from the sky like rain, that mankind will at the last remember our Lord and call his name but that the Lord will turn his face away. Those stories frightened me. I asked my grandmother if she was afraid of the destruction our Lord would bring upon us. She said that she was not and that she was looking forward to being in paradise. There, she said she would be together with all the children she had lost. There would be green pastures and indescribably beautiful music, such as we earthlings could not comprehend. Then she would embrace her little children that had passed away many years ago. She told me of the devil, that he is real and leads us into destruction, and that the blind will follow him but the love of God is much stronger and that at the end he will win. I then asked my grandmother what our Lord looked like. She told me that the Bible said he is the very likeness of us, for he is our Father. From that moment on religion had an impact on me.

I laid in bed trying to visualize our Lord. In my mind, I could see him as a huge powerful man in a white flowering robe with a bright halo about his head. He would sit like the king of all kings on a big throne made out of gold and jewels. His face was filled with utter kindness, his eyes radiating with love and understanding. The place he would sit upon, looking down on mankind, would be like a big hall made out of white marble and ivory. This is how I see our

Lord God to this day.

I had never met many of my relatives, especially not any on my father's side. My father's mother had passed on before I was born and his father when I was three. Of his other family, I knew only that he had two brothers, Albert, who lived in a distant city, and Ernst, who lived in Leipzig a province of Sachsen, with two sisters, Betty and Anny.

My grandmother had a daughter named Emmi who also resided in Memel, not very far from my grandmother's house. Being my mother's sister, of course she was my Aunt Emmi. Not long after I arrived in Memel she came to the house to meet me and to take me home with her. She was, in my opinion, a beautiful woman. She had a fair complexion, with rosy skin and blond and wavy hair. When we walked up to the apartment where she lived, I saw that it was an elegant new building with fancy glass in the entrance door. She lived on the second floor.

Her apartment was elegantly furnished. The dining room had a sturdy wooden table with matching chairs, and on the table was an elegantly laced tablecloth and fresh flowers. The couch was overstuffed, expensive looking, with fancy pillows made of velvet and lace. Her house looked very neat. There was nothing out of place.

Emmi was married but had no children. Her husband, Heinrich, was an officer in the Waffen SS[5]. When he arrived home that evening, he took my breath away. He entered the apartment wearing his full SS uniform. His officer's hat was decorated and looked important. He wore black rider's breeches with shiny, black high-topped boots and a black shirt. On his left arm, he wore the swastika armband. He smiled a hearty smile and greeted me with, "So, you are our niece, Rita?" He took me by the hand and

---

[5] This was the military branch of the dreaded SS. They fought in battle like any other German Army units, but were regarded as the elites. They also had higher than usual casualty rates.

led me into the living room.   There he sat on the couch and pulled me up on his knee.   He asked questions like how old I was, if I was enjoying my visit with my grandmother, and how long I planned to stay.

In contrast to my Aunt Emmi, who was a quiet introverted person, my uncle was very friendly, talkative and outgoing.   I liked him very much and he made me feel at ease.   He was tall and very handsome, with straight shiny teeth and had the appearance of always smiling. That was the first time I had met him and the last time as well.

I stayed with my Aunt Emmi a couple of days and was mostly impressed how very well she and her husband lived.

Going back to my grandmother's house again was like being home.   I had grown to love her very much.   Some evenings she would make braids all over my head and in the morning she would comb my hair and tell me how pretty I looked.

On warm afternoons my grandmother and I often walked to church.   There she would kneel at the last bench before walking into the house of God and pray.   Often I could see her lips move as she prayed.   After the service we would walk to the cemetery to visit the graves of her children.   There, by the graves, she would kneel again and pray.   Tears fell onto the sand where she knelt and prayed. That must have been very hard on her physically and emotionally for at night her legs would throb with pain until she moaned.

One afternoon my uncle Hermann asked if I wanted to go out for a stroll with him and that he would make it even more of pleasure and pull me in a wagon.   I had been afraid of him and always avoided him whenever possible.   I looked at my grandmother in hopes that she would not allow him to take me out.   To please him and avoid an angry outburst from him I told him I'd love to go in the wagon.

As I waited in the garden in front of the house, Hermann shuffled toward me pulling a small wagon made out of wooden boards. He told me to sit tight and he would pull me along. His right hand dangled lifeless by his side. I had hoped that he would not take me for a long walk for I could think of better things to do, like helping my grandmother in the garden, or collecting eggs from the few chickens that she owned.

As he pulled me along, he turned to the right onto a sandy walkway which was slightly uphill. He walked by beautiful gardens which were enclosed with white picket fences. The hill became steeper as he walked and the wagon was harder to pull. Suddenly he slipped on the sandy walkway and fell. He tried with all his strength to stand up, but it seemed to be impossible. As I sat there helplessly watching him struggle, he made another attempt. He reached out to the picket fence with his healthy arm and with all his might he struggled to get up. In the process, he broke several boards off the fence. His face had now broken out in a sweat, red colored, and angry.

The blue veins on his forehead were now protruding as if they would burst. The indentation in his forehead was pulsating very rapidly and I was afraid that he'd get angry and shout evil words at me. He made another attempt, breaking some more boards off the picket fence. This time he managed to pull himself up and stood on his two feet. I felt greatly relieved, but dared not look at him for the fear that he might curse at this unfortunate happening.

Going downhill toward home he insisted I sit in the wagon. I felt helpless and uneasy. I wished I could tell him to let me walk and pull the wagon so he could have better balance, but I dared not.

All too soon the time came that I had to leave Memel,

the beautiful garden town on the Kurisches Haff[6] by the Baltic Sea. Saying good-bye to my grandmother, looking into her beautiful old face, I could see that her eyes moistened when she hugged me. We told each other that we would be together again whenever it became possible.

---

[6] In English this is the "Curonian Lagoon".

Chapter 10

It felt good to be back at home in Osterode. There I could go swimming with Edith or visit our girlfriend, Helma Sontofski. She would then tell about all the experiences she had had with the witch Gamorra, such as the many times she appeared before her in the guise of a threat. Those stories were hair-raising and I loved them.

I could now go to the sand mountain and again fix up my castle that had by this time been completely destroyed by the winds. I could sit again and daydream, talk to our Heavenly Father and ask him to take care of my grandmother so that Hermann wouldn't lose his temper with her and make her cry. But most of all, I was looking forward to seeing my dear father coming home from Königsberg.

But now something had changed. My parents were always listening to the radio. Often there would be a speech by Adolf Hitler himself and my parents would listen with great intensity. Hitler's voice came over the radio very powerfully and loud, so that I could never understand what he was shouting. Every time he stopped shouting the people in the rally followed with floods of "Sieg Heil!"

Almost every household then had a picture of the

Führer hanging on the wall of the best room. There was a poster of Hitler hanging in every classroom of every school. At school he was mostly pictured with a child, holding a child in his arms, receiving flowers from a child, or holding one on his knee. I couldn't help but think that he loved children.

I will always remember those days. When my father now spoke of the future, he'd start with the words, "If we're still alive next year..." Then, he'd proceed to say what we would be doing or where we would travel to. I became worried and asked my father what he meant by saying "If we're still alive next year."

He took me between his knees. His blue eyes looked deep into mine, and he then told me that a big war was raging in the world, that the Russians were coming closer to the German border, especially from the east, very close to East Prussia, and that our future lay in the hands of our Führer. Because of the powerful shouting of our Führer I had confidence in him and knew that he would fight the Russians, and they would retreat back to where they belonged[7].

Being just 8 years old, I could not comprehend how serious the outlook for the future was. By then, there was an alarm system installed in Osterode, for when enemy planes were detected the alarm system would sound for everyone to take cover. The alarm system sounded somewhat like a fire alarm but the sirens had a deep and high sound slowly alternating. The siren made this horrible, loud, terrifying sound for one or two minutes. Whenever I heard the siren, I felt like the world was coming to an end and then I thought of the words my grandmother

---

[7] In fact, Rita's visit to Memel in 1942 was one of the last summers that the city remained in the hands of Germany. Starting in October 1944, most of the civilians of German ethnicity, including her relatives, were evacuated to other parts of Germany; four months later the city was captured.

had taught me, "God will punish us and send fire like rain from the heavens and that our Lord would speak to us with angry words of thunder and lightning, for he was angry for our greed." During these times I felt helpless and scared.

At some point after the alert the radio would then announce that Russian planes had passed our territory to drop bombs on Berlin and other large cities. This would be followed by the "All Clear" siren, which was a deep, long sound of relief. We in Osterode were never bombed.

When I grew into adulthood, thinking of my life the way it had evolved, I recognized three signs of the Lord had given us of a complete separation from my parents. The first was an incident with a neighbor, who was an invalided soldier with only one leg.

My mother, being a strong-headed East Prussian, had taken exception to a neighbor lady hanging her wash on the line too close to our front windows. Pouting and thinking about the thoughtlessness of this lady, she scooped ashes out of the kitchen stove, and with a bucket and a dust pan she proceeded to throw ashes on the lady's sheets to teach her a lesson not to block the view from our windows. The neighbor lady was of course angered about this, and sent her husband to our house to make the complaint for his wife.

He had served in the German Army as an SS officer, had lost one of his legs and was now a veteran, sent home to recover. Wearing his uniform, hobbling over on his crutches, he then in a mannerly way told my mother that she was wrong in soiling his wife's clean laundry. My mother, red in the face with anger, tried very hard to hold back some profanity but insisted that she was in the right. When the poor man turned on his crutches to go home my mother could not resist giving voice to her spite. Pretending to talk to herself, but speaking out loud to be sure he could hear her, and directed to his wife, she blurted,

"For the life of me, I can't understand why she has to send the cripple over to me." As the man walked away, he had heard the insult loud and clear.

It wasn't very long, in fact it was the next day, when we received a response to this insult, in the form of a visitor. It was another SS officer, but this one was on official business. He came into our house, looked around suspiciously and came right to the point. He told my mother that he had come in regard to the veteran officer that my mother had personally insulted, but what was worse, she had insulted the German uniform and thereby had committed treason. Mother was now beside herself and told the officer that she was truly sorry, that she did not mean it, and that she would apologize to the veteran.

The SS officer had in the meantime looked at every one of us children. We were all just standing there as if we were made out of clay. He then told my mother, as she sat motionless in a chair, her hands folded in her lap, with tears of sorrow pouring from her eyes, that she was a very lucky woman right then to have him answering the complaint, and not someone else. He told her that he had the authority to take her in that instant and not only that, he also told her (and I believe it was something he was not allowed to utter), she would in that case not be coming back. He told my mother that he, too, had little children and a wife and explained to my mother that we all have to be patriotic to win the war. I assume that he took into consideration the fact that my father was working in a defense plant and that our family was more than patriotic, and that my mother had her hands full with her four children, and had foolishly just lost her temper.

When he left my mother broke down and cried tears of joy, for she knew what she had done and realized the seriousness of her foolish insult.

Chapter 11

One day I heard the noise of machinery, and walking up to the sand mountain I was surprised with what I saw. Heavy equipment was uprooting and digging into the sand, building underground tunnels for a bomb shelter. As Edith and I stood and watched them work day after day; it did not take very long to complete the tunnel. It must have been a quarter of a mile long, and open on both ends.

On the inside, the walls were braced with straw boards to hold back the clay and insulate it from moisture. It was very dark in there. Walking from one end to the other there was not a ray of light until approaching the opening. The smell inside was moldy and muggy. I did not like the tunnel because it reminded me that the war was coming closer. In case of an air raid we now had to walk up to the sand hills to take cover and stay there until the siren sounded "all clear."

Now the news ordered all families to obtain gas masks. My mother one day walked into the house carrying in her hand six ugly gas masks. They came with complete instructions on how to use them. They were fabricated out of light grey rubber and fit over the entire face with a rubber band, like a diver's mask, to hold it on to the face. For the eyes there were two round glasses and the breathing apparatus was built with a filter which extended out from the face and looked monstrous. In case of a gas bomb attack, they would save lives and it was said, never to go into a shelter without a gas mask.

I thought to myself that I would never put such a monstrous looking device on my face, for the masked people looked as if they came from another world and were scary to look upon.

By now, the news was becoming more intense. Hitler's voice would scream over the loud speaker more and more. And in the background the people still shouted, "Sieg Heil!" It was now the fall of 1944. The little city of Osterode was enveloped with the brilliant colors of the season.

One day I heard singing and then silence, and then singing again. I asked Edith if she could hear what I thought I heard and she nodded her head yes. As we walked out to the street, from afar we could see the Army marching toward us. Our neighbors had already come out of their homes to view the spectacle. Now in endless chains they marched by, with a space between each troop. Alongside of each troop, off to the side, marched an officer, proudly holding his head high, his chest out, stomach in – which was their motto. His face was motionless and his eyes looked straight ahead into the destruction of his country. Every now and then the soldiers would break into a song as they marched. I remember that they were singing an old marching folk song:

"In the meadow
There blooms a flower
and its name is Erika."

Erika was also a popular name for girls. In English, Erika is *heather*. Another song, one inspired by Hitler, was:

"Today Germany belongs to us,
and tomorrow we will conquer the world."

By the time it was late November, my home was covered with snow. People were anxiously listening to the news on the radio which constantly reported our Army's position in the hot war going on to both the east and west. Hitler still screamed and promised the German people that the Army would fight up to the last man and that we would win the war. Most people had given up that hope. Stores were closing in the city and merchants were trying to sell out for just as much as people were willing to pay. Goods were sold for what seemed to be very little money, when they could be obtained, for what value was there in money when society itself seemed to be in danger? From that day forth the German mark steadily lost its value.

November passed, December arrived, and my little sister Waltraut turned four. This winter turned into the coldest winter I had yet seen, and the records agreed that it was one of the coldest in this century.

On January 12 the news was broadcast that the Russians had begun an offensive far to our south, almost 500 km away, directed apparently towards the middle of Poland. When my father arrived for the weekend, things seemed grimmer than usual with the news of the offensive, but even more ominous news was to come the next day, when we heard that they had also begun an offensive from their positions on the Narew River, headed in the direction of Osterode. And on the 14th the apparent final stage of the Soviet winter offensive began, as the Russian forces facing Königsberg, where our father worked, began a massive attack. When he left Sunday for work nothing much was said about things, at least in my hearing, but I

63

could feel the tension and the worry as if it were a great weight pressing down on us all. The following week dragged on with little to give us hope that things might reverse themselves.

Friday, January 19 came, and normally this would have been the day our father arrived home from Königsberg for the weekend, but the regularly scheduled train did not arrive. In the normally orderly German state this was a very disturbing development. What war news we got was confusing, and there were rumors of all kinds floating about, but we didn't know much for certain, like how close the Russians were and if they were getting any closer. There were some of our people who talked of the need to flee before they arrived, but apparently the authorities had forbidden this. Running away from the mercies of the Soviet Army was apparently "defeatist" and therefore treasonous.

On Saturday, my mother made a trip into town, and when she returned carrying beautiful dresses for all of us, she bragged about how cheaply she had acquired everything.

Part Two – Flight

Chapter 12

The next morning, on January 21, 1945 the radio announced that the Russian Army was breaking through the border. All mothers with their children were urged to evacuate to the west. A transport was being set up to accommodate everyone with mothers and children having priority.

Mother had prepared for flight by putting together a selection of necessities, with only the most urgently needed items. These were to be set at the curb of the street and were to be picked up and taken to the assigned train by the Hitler Youth. Accordingly, she placed our few belongings at the curb and now we had walked to the train station to wait for the train from Königsberg with hopes that our father would arrive with it.

We arrived to find that the train station was in turmoil. There were crowds waiting to meet their assigned trains to flee from the Russians with hopes of coming back home as soon as their Hitler had driven off the Russians.

Suddenly, my mother spotted my father getting off the train. She ran toward him and kissed him. He put his arm around her and they walked over to where we were standing. Relieved to have him with us we walked home for the last time. When we arrived back home we found that the Hitler Youth had still not arrived to take our belongings to the train station.

We walked into the house one last time, and while adding some of Papas belongings to our kit, it was decided that we would take all the treasures that we had to leave behind and hide them in the crown of our big stove in the living room. I can't remember all the things that fit inside the crown, but I remember so well that my beautiful roller scooter was placed there. Oh, if I could just take that one thing with me, but I knew not to ask. My father explained,

"If we should live to come back one day we may then find the things that we loved but had to leave behind."

It was getting late and the Hitler Youth had failed to show. So mother and father took our sled and placed our meager belongings there, together with my two younger sisters who were 4 and 6 years old.

When we arrived back at the train station there were people swarming like bees. Single people and old people had to step back and give priority to families with children. We were assigned to a boxcar on an enclosed freight train, which was lined with straw for warmth. My parents placed our sled against the wall of the train. They sat us together on the straw and covered us with the blankets we had taken with us. I remember there were gas masks hanging above our heads on the train. I had no idea as to our designation but I felt secure for I knew my father was with us and that he knew.

Our train set in motion and rolled out of the station leaving behind many people. Those in the boxcar were talking with each other softly, some even cried.

My parents had a conversation with a young lady named Grete, who was a pretty young woman with a face like in a fairytale. Her skin was rosy and her smile enhanced her face by showing beautiful white teeth. She had blond hair which had been braided and laid around her head. Short, curly locks decorated her face, giving her a youthful girlish look. She was 24 years old.

She was with her elderly parents, and explained to my parents that her father owned a bakery business and that he had worked hard all his life building his business. But now he was 84 years old, sick and feeble, and they didn't know what would become of him. He did not know where he was or what was going on at that point.

The train rolled on for a few hours but then suddenly stopped. No one knew what had happened and why the train was not moving. Evening came and still we sat. Finally, at daybreak, the big freight gave a jerk and slowly started to roll again. By that time, the 84 year old man was critically ill. His 74 year-old wife sat by him and watched as he breathed the last breath of life. She shed some tears and her young daughter, Grete, comforted her in the loss of her life companion. Grete did not cry. She said that her father would not have reached our destination, that he was too ill, and it was best for him just to pass on.

Quickly all the people in our boxcar were aware that a person had just died and they decided to dispose of the dead man by sliding open the boxcar door and throwing the body out into the snow while the train was in motion. Sitting not too far from the door I could observe the whole process. Two men, one holding the old man by the shoulders and the other by the feet let the old man fall out the door while the train rolled down the tracks into nowhere. Then they shut the door and no one talked of it again.

It wasn't long afterwards that the train slowed down and again came to a halt. We had no idea why, and likewise no way to know how long it would wait. Since there were no toilet facilities in the cars, many people now had the urge to seek a private place to relieve themselves. Some did what they had to do near the tracks, and we had a pail in our car that someone had brought for the purpose, but my mother told my father that she must get off the train. He pleaded with her to stay on the train and use the pail, but she would not hear of it and insisted that she get off. Others in the car also advised against it, because the train could start up at any moment. But she was stubborn, and stepped off the train anyway.

Father wanted to be there to help her if the train started moving, and so went with her. They started to walk down into an embankment to be hidden from the view of people. I remember that I had been worried and was hoping they would not wander off too far.

Then with a jerk the train started slowly rolling. There was no sight of my parents. The people in our boxcar called out to them, that they must hurry. All of us children were now crying hysterically for our parents. The train started to roll faster and suddenly they appeared in the distance. My father, holding my mother by the hand, tried to run as fast as he could, dragging her behind him and pulling her along. The train had now reached a dangerous speed and the people in our boxcar were calling out to them to hurry. Agony was visible in their faces as they called out to them to run.

They could not reach the boxcar we were in, but with effort managed to get to a car further back in the train, where father put his hands around mother's waist, telling her to grab onto the handhold and pull herself up. Now she was safely on the train. My father, in the meantime, grabbed onto the iron handhold and held on for his life. Then with a swing he stood on the platform and he, too, was safe.

We were screaming with terror and despair, hoping that they had made it, for if they had not made it we would be going out into nowhere without our parents and surely would have lost them forever.

As soon as the people who were rooting for them to race the train observed they were safe, they turned to us children and announced that they had made it safely back with us. My parents now occupied another boxcar but we all felt relieved to have them with us again. When the train came to a halt once more my parents hurriedly joined us in our boxcar. This was the second sign we had been given that our parents could be lost to us.

As we traveled along, it became night. We were huddled together like cattle in the freight train. The snow covered the countryside, and it was cold and clammy. My parents continued to converse the beautiful young girl who had just lost her father, whose body lay somewhere behind us in the snow, down an embankment. We had no light of any kind in the boxcar and soon I dozed off. With a mighty jerk, throwing people from one end of the car to another, the train screeched and came to a halt once more.

The people now felt confused and bewildered. Some indicated that we might have had a collision. They opened our boxcar door and stretched their necks to see if they could determine what had gone wrong. Some of the men, including my father, stepped off the train to investigate. Soon my father appeared and told us what happened. He told us that there had been a collision between a Red Cross train carrying wounded soldiers and another freight train carrying evacuated refugees like us. Our train had managed to stop just before hitting the freight ahead of us. He told my mother to stay in the boxcar, that he and the other men from other boxcars were helping with the dead and wounded.

When my father returned he explained to us and the other people that our situation was hopeless and that the train could not proceed any further. The tracks were damaged and the dead and wounded were thrown all about the area. People started to rustle restlessly, whispering to each other in despair. Children were crying and their parents felt helpless. My parents moved out the sled, folded our blankets and took one small suitcase. They sat my two little sisters on the sled and wrapped them in blankets. We now had to walk. As we were ready to leave the miserable boxcar, the young woman, Grete, pleaded with my mother to take her along. When my parents asked about her 74-year-old mother she told them that her mother said that it was hopeless and that she'd have to leave her behind. Also that she was too old to endure the stress any longer. My parents assured her that she could go with us, wherever that may be.

Chapter 13

Edith and I walked in front of our parents while Grete walked beside them and my father pulled the sled carrying Irmgard and Waltraut. The night was damp and very cold. The snow was quite deep along the way, which made the walking even more difficult. We must have walked two hours when I could see the breaking of dawn. My mother started to complain that she felt frozen all over her body and could not feel any circulation in her feet. My father replied that as soon as we could spot some light in the distance that meant there would be town or a farmhouse, and we could stop there for a time. As we walked my mother complained of the cold even more.

It wasn't long before we spotted a light in the distance, and as we approached it we saw that it was farm. When we knocked at the farmhouse door and asked the people there for help, they were friendly and receptive, letting us in to get warm. Inquiring about our whereabouts they informed us that we were now at the outskirts of the town of Prussian Holland, meaning that after all this train travel we were still only about 60 kilometers from our home. As we walked into the large farmhouse, there were several other people already there, stranded just like us.

My father asked for a pan to rub our feet with snow to

start the circulation in our feet.   When he was done and had dried our feet with a towel, he asked the people if he could use the phone to ask the German Red Cross if there was another train traveling west.   They shook their heads no, and said that all communications were out – the telephone lines were all dead.   There was nothing more for it but to rest and warm our bodies for a time before setting out again. When we did, it was daylight.

As we set out my parents arranged us as before, with the two little ones on the sled and Edith and I marching ahead.   We were still hoping to find a train that would take us to safety, so we continued into the city of Prussian Holland.   The road into town was filled with wagons as far as the eyes could see.   There was an endless chain of people sitting in their horse-drawn wagons.   Their belongings, such as pails and bundles, dangled from the sides of their wagons.   Most of the wagons were covered with canvas, just as you see it in Western movies when the people try to immigrate to California for the gold rush.   Some wagons had a cow tied to them or even an extra horse, and some of the people even had their pet dog walking alongside their wagon.

Crossing the road was utterly impossible because the mass of wagons wouldn't stop and trying to cross was to take a chance of being trampled to death by their horses.   So we simply joined the stream of refugees. By now, I held on to my father's hand, for if I did not pay attention to whom I belonged I could get lost in the sea of people.

Behind us in the distance, I could hear gun and cannon fire and thought that the German army must be fighting back against the Russians[8].   The gunfire became louder and more intense.   It sounded like the explosion of

---

[8] This was actually the sound of Russian tanks firing on the refugees at the Grünhagen train station, where the train wreck had occurred.

guns, bombs, and grenades. By now, I feared that we could be struck by a grenade or a machine gun bullet. I pleaded with my father to please find a house and take cover. My father did not answer, but held my hand even tighter, and we kept walking together with the other people on the road.

There was an intensification of the sounds of battle, until it sounded as if they were shooting directly at us. I cried and asked my father to please take cover in a house, any house. My mother joined with me in insisting that we find shelter, whereupon my father then led us off the road and we walked toward a house.

My father knocked on the door, but there was no answer. He then tried the doorknob, but the door had been left locked by the owners. The sound of guns and explosions now seemed to sound like it was happening all around us, like thunder in its worst stage. My father then broke some glass in the door and turning the handle from the inside opened the door. Once inside the sounds were muffled, and I felt that we were now safe, and to be even safer I could always hide under the bed or in some dark corner.

The house inside was quite empty of people. It was clear that the people who had lived there were rich and had some very nice things. The bedroom furniture was of the finest quality, there were satin quilted spreads on their beds and everything was clean and elegant. All the other rooms were the same. There were expensive paintings on the walls and other valuable things about the house. The bathroom was very modern, with a built-in bathtub and tiled walls. The kitchen was large and the walls there likewise covered with white ceramic tile. The kitchen had an ultra-modern white enameled stove.

When my father investigated who the owners of that beautiful house were, he found that it belonged to a master chimney sweep, the man who employed all the chimneysweeps in that town.

As a child, I remembered chimney sweeps. They used to wear a black uniform with a top hat (for a master) or a round cap just covering the middle of their head (for the journeymen). Around their waist they carried a heavy iron ball on a chain and at the opposite side of the lead ball would be a circular wire brush to sweep the soot down, if there were any. When the chimney sweep came to clean the chimney or chimneys of the apartment house, he would first stand in the courtyard and shout loud and clear that he was now sweeping the chimney. When the inhabitants heard this they would shut the flues in their living room heating units.

It was about this time that an old man named Klein joined us. I didn't remember this until my mother reminded me of it years later, but Herr Klein had entered the house not long after we did, and my parents told him he was welcome to stay with us.

It turned out that he was from my parents' hometown Memel, had been evacuated to Prussian Holland with his wife several months before Memel was captured. He and his wife had been quartered with the family that lived in this house, but that they had both been hospitalized not long before. His wife had since died in the hospital, and when the staff fled, he decided to return to this house. He was not very well, and was very quiet, so I had no memories of him, until sometime later.

Now that we were in the house, and sat down in the bedroom of the house, my mother told us children to close our eyes and try to sleep on the big bed. I was nervous and I did not know what would happen on the next day. My parents and Grete, now a member of the family, were trying to shut their eyes while sitting on the soft chairs. The sounds of battle never stopped, but we were very tired from our journey so far, so we slept some hours on the nice comfortable bed. When dawn arrived mother awakened us

74

children.

When my parents looked out the bedroom window, they saw that many of the houses in the neighborhood had white flags hanging out of their windows. There were many houses in flames and Russian tanks were rolling into the city. Quickly my parents hurried to hang white sheets from all the windows, to show the Russians that we surrendered to them.

Oh my God, I prayed, please don't let the Russians shoot us now. Where was Adolf Hitler, I thought, and why did he not scream over the loud speakers that he would defeat the Russians? I could not bear the thought that my dear parents, my sisters whom I loved so and myself could all be shot in just a very little while, maybe an hour? Or maybe as long as two hours?

Chapter 14

I stood stiff as if frozen to the floor. "Where could I hide?" I wondered; but I thought that all of us should find a place to hide. I had no idea what thoughts my parents were having but they must have been similar to mine. Silently we waited. Our flags were hanging out the windows, showing the Russians that there were Germans in the house and not offering resistance.

Now more and more tanks were coming. And finally there were Russian soldiers walking toward the houses. Oh, my God, there they were. My father had unlocked and opened the latch on the door to show them that we were not resisting them.

They approached with their machine guns pointed toward the house and as they came to the front door they pushed it open with the barrels of their weapons. Four or five of them walked in, and my parents and Grete stood with their hands above their heads. With guns pointed at us the soldiers asked us if we owned the house. My father, thank God, had learned the Russian language from the White Russian prisoners in the defense plant, so he was able to answer them in their language. When they heard him speak their language they asked if we were Bolshevists.

My parents nodded yes[9]. Of course, my parents were no such thing (Hitler would have had them shot), but it was safest to seem like friends to them.

One of the soldiers walked over to my mother and with a jerk of his hand he pulled her earrings right out of her ears. Her earrings were pierced through her ears with a gold wire and a ruby hanging down from her ears. He then took the watch from her arm and asked if there was any more jewelry and that we must hand it over.

My father explained that the house did not belong to us, so we didn't know, so while one of the soldiers held us at gunpoint, the others proceeded to ransack the house. Pictures were flying off the walls, furniture was overturned, and after they pulled out all the drawers they spilled oil on the white linens and stepped on the things that were breakable.

As they moved through the house, they talked very loud and boisterously, making sure they entered every room. They seemed angry about everything their eyes came across. Once they found pictures of the family that had lived there they were now convinced that we were telling the truth about not being the capitalists that owned the house, which was good. As they continued to smash and break everything that signified riches, it seemed the main purpose of their looting was locating all the jewelry they could find. Everything else of value that couldn't be easily carried off was destroyed.

The whole place was in shambles by the time they left.

Afterwards, more Russians came into the house, maybe three or four. They all looked the same, with dark brown uniform coveralls, quilted jackets and quilted heavy

---

[9] Bolshevism was adopted by Lenin from the theory of the German Socialist, Karl Marx. It is also called Leninism, and we know it as Communism.

hats that only the tank soldiers wore. Their hats made them frightening to me, and I knew that with their guns could shoot us at any time they pleased. The second group of Russians also searched the house quickly, trashing the house still more, and they too asked us if we were the capitalists who lived there. My father again explained that we had only taken shelter there and that the house did not belong to us.

All the Russians who came through that day were concerned about whether we were Bolsheviks or Capitalists. Being eight years old, I could not understand the meaning of the two words. I concluded that it must mean whether we were good or bad Germans. All during these visitations, my father continued to stand in the same place, answering every question the soldiers asked him in fluent Russian. I could see in his face that everything was all right. I believed my father saved our lives by being able to speak their language.

And the soldiers were very mistrustful about the food and drink they found, as if they were afraid it had been poisoned. They wouldn't touch the food, but when they found wine or cognac, they asked my father to open the bottle and taste the contents so they could be sure it was safe to drink.

The very first Russians to march into East Prussia were Mongols from the region of Siberia, Russians from the Ukraine, the Baikal and Belorussia. They were primitive people and many had never seen a house that had multiple rooms with rich-looking furniture in every one of them. They could not comprehend that people ate, slept, and lived in separate quarters of the house. They had never seen a bathroom with a built in bathtub and even more, they were mystified by the toilet, and by flushing.

The toilet in this house was in the modern style, with the water tank installed high up on the wall just under the ceiling, having a lever actuator with a chain hanging from it. When the handle at the end of the chain was pulled, this would cause the tank to empty down the pipe to the toilet, thus flushing its contents into the sewer pipes.

But because the water supply was cut off due to the battle, when one of the soldiers pulled the chain to see what would happen, it only made a loud gurgling noise, causing them all to flee temporarily out of the house, for fear something might explode. This would have been funny under other circumstances, but these men carried machine guns and in their fear might have killed us all.

After many groups of Russian soldiers had gone through the house looking for loot or searching for armed enemies, now a Russian officer came into the house. He approached the grown-ups and asked many questions about where we came from and whether we belonged to the Nazi regime. My father answered all the questions in our favor and the officer seemed to be pleased.

His uniform was clean and pressed. His shoulder straps were braided with gold stripes. His hat was flat brown with a brown visor, braided with a gold band and in the center there was the symbol of Soviet power, a red star.

He was a cultured and educated man, and introduced himself as Colonel Shakirov. He told my father that his troops would occupy the house and the ground around the house. He instructed my mother that she would cook for his men and as long as he was in charge of the area he would also protect our family. But he told my parents that after his troops left we would be again on our own and unprotected.

So my mother busied herself and lighted the big white stove and had a hot coal fire going in the kitchen. There was no running water to cook or wash with, so we had to gather many pails of snow which had to be melted for use. The meals she had to prepare consisted mainly of what was called *kasha*, a favorite Russian food, which is porridge made from buckwheat or a number of other grains like cereal wheat, barley, oats, millet or rye. It was cooked in a big kettle and was served inside the house to six to eight soldiers of higher rank.

The Russians would seat themselves at the large table and eat their *kasha* with bread. The first time when they were finished and had left the table Edith and I walked into the room in hopes of finding some leftovers for us. But all we could find on the table was a mess of something I could not recognize. The food looked so unsightly that no matter how hungry we were we could not eat any.

There was a big kettle with some leftover food, which had wine poured into it. It also contained paper and bits of fat meat. The bread had also been soaked with wine and mashed into the porridge and was topped with cigarette butts and ashes. I thought to myself that a hog wouldn't be able to eat food like that. Nothing could be salvaged.

Every time the Russians had a meal in that room it was always the same. The food had been ruined. I concluded that it was done purposely so that we Germans could not live off the army and eat their food.

Chapter 15

Colonel Shakirov had told my parents that we would be protected while his unit was using the house, and we were. But the protection didn't cover us all equally. This became clear only a few days after their arrival.

A soldier walked into the bedroom that we occupied, pointing a pistol at Grete and told her in broken German to come with him. Grete, with a frightened expression on her face, looked worriedly at my father and then at my mother.

The soldier held the pistol to her head nodded his head toward the door, motioning her to go with him. I did not understand and my thought was that he wanted to shoot the pretty young woman. When Grete appeared again I was happy to see her back again. She threw her arms around my mother and cried bitterly. My mother comforted her by saying that she must be glad to be alive.

It wasn't long before another soldier came and made the same advances. Grete was now distraught and disillusioned and tried to defend herself by disguising herself as an old woman. She dressed in black clothing, hid her hair under a grandmotherly scarf and built a humpback into her blouse to make her look ancient. But it was no use. The news must have traveled among the soldiers that there was a beautiful young girl living in the house, for it wasn't long before another soldier appeared at the premises pointing his weapon at her. He walked toward her, pulled the scarf off her head and told her to come with him. As my parents stood powerless he pushed her out of the door and they disappeared.

By now I understood that the pretty young girl was being raped by many soldiers. She tried desperately to find a place to hide, but it seemed useless. In spite of our incredible luck to be alive, my mother had now developed a hatred toward the soldiers. One day she had just hidden Grete under the bed when a very young soldier walked into our room. He looked as if he was barely 17 years of age. Asking for the young fräulein, he was told that she was not with us any longer. He then reached for his pistol and walked over to my mother and told her to come with him. My father stood motionless and could not protect her, but she stood still within reach of the soldier and did not move. Her face reddening from anger, her eyes flashing with hate, she made her hand into a fist, and waving at him she told him in half Lithuanian and half Russian that he was nothing but a snot-nose boy, that she could be his mother, and that if he did not disappear in a flash that she would call Colonel Shakirov and report to him what was happening.

This young Russian might not have been able to understand everything she had said, but he did understand that she wasn't going to surrender to his advances, that she was angry and most of all, that she knew his commanding officer by name. Immediately he turned on his heels and left the room. My mother again had taken a step into the unknown and survived. Many women, their husbands, and their whole families were shot because they resisted the Russians.

The only food we had was whatever we could find in the house. There were potatoes in the cellar and flour and lard in the kitchen cabinets. We never had to share this food with the Russians because they would not eat anything except for the food they received from their own supplies. They would not eat from us and we could never salvage any of their food.

It still sounded every day like there was a war going on: we could hear guns sounding in the distance, and it sounded like the German army was still trying to fight back the Russians.

And here in Prussian Holland there were houses all around ours being set on fire. Fortunately, we had a whole company of Russian soldiers occupying the field around our house and that is why our house had been spared. So here we lived from day to day, not knowing what catastrophe would befall us tomorrow.

One morning, something woke me when it was still very early. The room was still and everyone slept the sleep of the despairing. The old clock on the credenza ticked away the time. This clock would sound every hour with a beautiful melody which I can still remember today. And now this morning it gonged the time. It was 5:00 a.m.

As I lay in bed, crowded by my parents and sisters, I noticed that I could not see Grete sleeping anywhere in the room. I looked around, thinking she might be hiding under the bed, but not finding her there, I searched in the kitchen and other rooms. As I walked into the bathroom, there was Grete hanging from the ceiling with a rope tied around her neck. Her head had fallen to the side, her face in the twilight looked bluish white like the snow at the break of dawn. As I stood there staring at the figure, I could see no movement, but thinking that she might still be alive, I hurried and awakened my mother. Together with my father she cut Grete down. They laid her down on the bed, massaged her heart and tried to revive her. My mother could detect a pulse. They knew that she would live.

Grete rested and in a day had fully recovered. My

parents tried hard to hide her away from the Russian soldiers. They built a shelter for her in the darkest corner of the cellar, for the Russians were afraid of the dark and would not venture there without a torch or other light. This shelter was built out of coal briquettes, which were the size and shape of building bricks, and could be neatly stacked, and they made a small opening for her to slip in and out of. It seemed that Grete would be safe there. To conceal the hideaway, they piled cut wood over the briquettes and made it inconspicuous. Grete had blankets in there to keep her warm and she ended up staying there in the cellar for as long as we remained in the house.

Day to day life for us children was pretty simple, and we only had one simple task, which was to obtain snow that could be melted for drinking and cooking. Otherwise there wasn't much for us to do.

I saw that no matter where they went, Russian soldiers always carried their weapons with them. This seemed dangerous and scary to us, but some of the soldiers became friendly, especially to us children. My youngest sister, Waltraut, had recently turned four and Irmgard, six. Both had had a birthday in December. The soldiers paid great attention to them, especially to the youngest, Waltraut. She was a pretty little girl with thick blond hair and big blue eyes. When she smiled deep dimples appeared on her cheeks, and she gave the appearance of a china doll. When the Russians set her up on their knees they would call her "*malenkiy kukla*," which means "little doll".

One soldier told my father that he, too, had a family, but had not seen his children in many years. Others told us that they had not seen their homes for as long as 12 years. These were the condemned Russians who had committed some crime and together, with their families, had been exiled to the wasteland of Siberia or to the Ural Mountains. There they would have to live for the rest of their lives. It was the plan of the government to populate that region and develop the land. That is why so many Russian soldiers were pleased at the sight of a tiny baby-like child. They would stroke her hair and talk to her in their language, which she could not understand. When she laughed they would laugh and they were overjoyed by her response.

One soldier gave Waltraut the most precious thing he had acquired for himself, a gold watch. He placed the watch on her wrist and showed her how to listen to the ticking. Then he watched her face for her joyful reaction. When she smiled he told her that it was hers and that she was to keep it. The next soldier was amazed that such a little child had a gold watch and took it away from her.

Chapter 16

We had originally taken shelter in the house on January 23, and about two weeks had gone by. We were surprisingly still alive and had stayed together for all that time. Things were about to change, however.

Colonel Shakirov walked into our quarters, took my parents aside and talked with them extensively. After this long discussion he walked away. With blank looks on their faces our parents now told us that we had two hours to clear out of the house. We could only take with us the most needed items, such as our clothes and some food.

The officer had explained to my father that his unit was moving on and that we had to make room for the next unit, which would likewise occupy the entire house and the ground around it. The new unit did not want to have us stay with the house.

Grete was told to dismantle the hideout in the cellar, for it must be kept a secret why she was not found, that we had deliberately hid her.

My father found a baby carriage into which we placed the essentials, like all the food it would hold. Within two hours we walked away in search of a new roof over our heads. As we walked along the streets, we saw no German people. The streets looked uprooted and littered with clothes, papers, and fallen bricks from burned buildings. There were many tanks standing along the side of the road with the red star of the Russian army painted on them. Russian combat trucks drove up and down the city. The air smelled foul with motor oil. My parents had to find shelter soon for they knew it was dangerous to walk far.

As we turned into a side street my mother said to my father, "Oh, let's try this house." It was a three story grey building. As we walked up a flight of stairs a dog started to bark. My father knocked at the door and a voice of an old lady asked what we wanted. My father spoke through the door and said that we were looking for shelter. He asked if there was room for us. The dog was barking so furiously that we could not hear what the old woman answered. Suddenly the door opened and an old, grey haired lady peeked out her head. As she spoke to us the dog snarled tried to attack, barking fiercely. My mother, still standing on the landing of the stairway, called out to my father that she did not want to live in that house, and that we should find another place.

Our family then walked down the stairs and proceeded to look for something else. We came to a sturdy building made of red brick. The front of it looked like a store. The inside had been ransacked and burned. Alongside the store front we found the ground floor entrance to a dwelling on the second floor. As we walked up the wide, red, painted wooden steps, we came upon a big entrance door. We walked into the house. It looked looted and deserted, but everything was intact.

There was no broken furniture in these rooms. A big double sliding door was the entrance to a large, roomy bedroom with all the bed clothing intact. Against a wall stood a large chifferobe which contained a man's and a lady's clothing. Next to the white tile heating stood a comfortable, overstuffed chair. Off the bedroom was an ultra-modern bathroom with a built-in bathtub with green tile walls, and no window. Since there was no electricity in the city the only light in the bathroom was from the open door. The bathroom had some light due to far window of the bedroom. Since our only water supply was melting snow, the nice bathroom was of no use to us.

We wondered at the identity of the owners of the house, who also apparently owned the furniture and coffin manufacturing firm whose storefront was downstairs, with their factory standing in the back of the building. Again, we had landed in the undesirable home of a capitalist. We later found out that the owners had lived in the villa across the street from the chimneysweep's house, and that this was their townhouse. And we also found out that they had died during the Soviet onslaught.

By some coincidence there was already an occupant of these premises, someone whom we already knew, and that was a Herr Klein, who had been with us briefly at the chimneysweep house. I didn't remember him from there, but many years later mother told about how he had showed up there shortly after we took shelter – but he must have moved on to the main part of town, because I have no memory of him before we came to this next building. He welcomed us, but claimed the chair by the stove as his own, by virtue of his age, and of course we accommodated him. My parents looked around the establishment and found it had many rooms. We acquired a table and placed it in front of the large window next to our bed. There we would sit, eat, and plan for the next day, but no one spoke of the future for we had no future for many years to come.

Outside the window, I could see the big red brick building of what had been the manufacturing company. The house had a corridor which connected the living quarters with the factory, and so Edith and I went to investigate. In the factory, we found big planks of

88

unfinished wood and in a separate section, there were unfinished wooden coffins, big ones as well as little ones. Looking at the coffins, I was overcome with a ghostly feeling and wanted to leave.

As I walked back into the house, I saw a Russian dressed in a tanker's uniform in the living room. His big quilted hat reminded me of a soldier who had come to destroy and burn cities. He looked angry, asking again if we were the capitalists. My father assured him that we were not. Throwing and breaking paintings, he left, but not failing first to take a good look at Grete.

The next morning I was awakened by some kind of turmoil taking place in our very room. As I raised my head, I could see the tank soldier throwing himself at Grete. The whole room smelled of foul machine oil. With his terrible large quilted hat he was struggling with Grete right in front of my eyes. Grete was screaming and trying to fight him off. My mother told us children to look the other way, but by that time I knew Grete was being raped.

Again, we made a shelter for Grete in the cellar. The cellar in that house was far from the living quarters and looked like a dungeon. It was so dark one could not see one's hand in front of his or her eyes, and the floor consisted of black dirt. There was heating material, coal, and split wood; but it was very cold and clammy. I knew Grete was afraid to stay there. I thought to myself, "Why can't Grete be a child like us? Why must she be so very beautiful and young? Her beauty is against her." My mother was 32 and had my father for protection, not because he was her husband, but because he spoke fluent Russian. The primitive soldiers, after he told them he was a Bolshevik, thought he was on their side, and some even wanted to be friends. Unfortunately, he could do nothing to prevent their attacks on Grete.

Not long thereafter, one night I got up to hear a rustling in the green bathroom. I stood still to listen and then heard a croaking, rasping noise. As my eyes searched the room, there in the corner I could see Grete huddled on the floor, her hands clasped together over her chest, her eyes glazed as if she were semiconscious. I asked her what was the matter with her and she croaked again. I knew then that she could not speak.

I ran into the bedroom, calling for my mother. She carried Grete into the room and laid her on the bed. Grete had swallowed some acid she had found – it must have been in the furniture factory. It was acetic acid, the kind you make vinegar from. Sticking her finger down Grete's throat, my mother induced her to vomit. Then my mother boiled tea and poured it down Grete's throat, as much as Grete could take, then she made Grete vomit again and again. Grete had tried to kill herself once more, this time by burning her insides with acid. Slowly she recovered her voice, but was left permanently hoarse. From then on, while the Russians still came often, Grete lived in the dungeon of the cellar where she would remain safe.

As horrible as things were for Grete, the soldiers always smiled and talked friendly with us children. My baby sister had been given presents by the soldiers, and they would hold her on their laps and feed her their food. It was clear that they would not hurt children.

There were some who brought their musical instruments when they came to visit. They loved playing the stringed instrument called the balalaika and also the accordion. Their songs had sad melodies and their lyrics spoke of longing for their loved ones and their homeland. The ones we were dealing with now were Russians from the Baikal region. Their melodies reflected the emptiness and the extreme cold and loneliness of their country.

One day, my mother told Edith and I that a Russian patrol officer had relayed an order that the adults in our family register themselves with the Russian Commandant. It was imperative because that Russians wanted to determine the population of German people living in East Prussia. So on that day, February 13, 1945, my parents dressed warm to make the trip. My mother wore a dark grey wool overcoat with a light grey Persian lamb collar. Her dark wavy hair was combed back and tied in a ponytail. My father wore a dark blue overcoat with a scarf tied around his neck and his head was bare. He told my mother to bring all the records of their birth, marriage and the birth records of all the children. He told us children to remain in the house, that it was better that we stayed home for there might be many people coming to register, and that the process with all the red tape could drag out until dark. Herr Klein, sitting comfortably in the chair, nodded his head approvingly; apparently he was too old to be required to register. Grete was still in the cellar; although she was required to register, too, she would not leave.

Edith and I decided to take the baby buggy and go back to the chimney sweeper house to see if we could bring back some of the food that we had left behind; my mother said that she had left a cheese wheel in the attic of the house. By now, we had learned that children did not have to fear the Russian soldiers. Riding by in their combat trucks, they would wave at us and with a smile shout words we could not understand. So off we went.

But our journey was fruitless. Arriving at our previous home we were not allowed to enter. When we tried to approach the house, a Russian officer had motioned to us that we should get off the premises and walk away. Walking home, we passed the old grey house that we had approached once to find quarters, the one with the barking dog. To my dismay it was burned to the ground. As I walked into the hollow shell, there was the dog lying in the rubble. His fur looked singed from the heat and his body was stiff and rigid. Farther off to the side there was the old woman lying among the fallen bricks and ashes. I told Edith that our God in heaven had warned us through the dog, for he had saved our lives. Arriving home, we saw the evening sun make its last attempt to shine its golden rays upon our pitiful city.

Chapter 17

In the morning ur parents had still not returned home.

By now our food consisted only of bread and lard. We had to conserve our water, which we boiled daily, melting it from snow. There was not any water for bathing. We were also now suffering from head and clothing lice.

Edith and I kept ourselves busy combing each other's hair to rid ourselves of the head lice that constantly caused our scalps to itch. It began to get late and it was dark outside when I asked Herr Klein what might have happened to our parents and why they were not back when it was dark. He just shrugged his shoulders and said not to worry.

Waking up the next morning, I was overcome by a scary feeling of emptiness. It was the first time I had felt afraid and alone. I shook Edith by the shoulders and told her to wake up, that our parents had not come back. Edith sat up in her bed, looked around and said, "They might come home today." That day we never left the premises, but waited.

The chifferobe in our bedroom stood on legs, and so under it our parents had stored our bread wrapped in paper for each of us to eat. On the bread we spread the lard and for taste we sprinkled it with salt. We had no water and the snow outside had melted away. Again, we made it a daily practice to keep the insects out of our clothing and also our hair. Irmgard, my younger sister, by now had developed open sores on the scalp of her head from the lice. She scratched her head constantly and the sores started to bleed and get crusty.

My parents were still gone. Herr Klein was the only adult we had with us, but he was a man of few words and always sat like a statue in the big chair by the stove. We had not seen Grete for several days, since she had made her home in the dark cellar. So the adults were of no help to us children for the unspoken motto was "do not concern yourself with others, but run for your own life."

Edith was now 11 years, and I was the second oldest at 8. Although Edith looked the tallest and strongest of us four girls, I was little for my age, and very thin. I could have been mistaken for a little girl of 6, and if anyone had seen them, my rib seemed to be covered by skin only, for they protruded and were very visible. My arms and legs were also very thin-looking, but despite appearances I felt quite healthy and wiry.

So, being the oldest, Edith now took charge and began making all the decisions. Her first decision was that we would not share our bread and lard with Herr Klein; if Herr Klein wanted to eat, he would have to come by his own food.

We were carefully rationing our bread and lard, only eating a little each day, and Edith had told Herr Klein that he was not to eat our food, since it had been collected by our parents for our family, and that he must seek his own. But he ignored this, and ate from our food regardless. When Edith reminded him that he had to find his own food, he answered that she was only a child and must never talk disrespectfully to a grown-up. He threatened that if she continued to be disrespectful he would have to use his cane on her for discipline.

Our parents were lost to us for over two weeks when Edith and I decided to look for them in every possible way. Edith decided that all four of us would go to the Russian Commandant and ask to speak to the commander of the whereabouts of our parents. As the four of us approached the big building of the Russian headquarters, we saw that the entrance door was guarded by two soldiers with fixed bayonets. When we stood before the door, Edith asked to speak with the commander; but the soldiers just smiled at us. She persisted again and again, with no action on their part – they obviously could not understand what we wanted. As other soldiers walked in and out of the entrance on business, one of the guards asked one of them what our intentions were.

This one stood there a moment, looking at us. Then with a serious face he turned around and disappeared into the entrance. A few minutes later he reappeared, but with the officer who was a commander of the Russian Army. The soldiers on guard and standing around immediately stood at attention. His uniform was decorated with many medals hanging from his shirt pocket. He wore no hat, his hair was dark blonde and wavy. His face was friendly and while he looked down on us with a smile he asked in broken German what we wanted of him.

Edith proceeded to explain that our parents had been asked by a Russian patrol soldier to come to the headquarters and register their names and that they had not been seen or heard from for over two weeks. As he heard the question, his face took on a grimmer aspect.

The commander looked at all of us and said that Hitler had destroyed many thousands of families in his country, had shot and killed many of his comrades, had killed their children and destroyed the cities. Hitler had done damage that would take many years to correct. He said that now the German people must pay their debt. He told us to go home and regard the loss of our mother and father as the debt we owed to Russia and that it was an aspect of the war. As he spoke to us children, his voice became louder, as if he were angered. With that, he turned around and walked back into the building.

We walked disconsolately back to the house, and when we arrived we found Grete in our bedroom sitting on the bed. Both of her arms were bandaged, red blood seeping through the bandages. She had once again tried to end her life, this time by cutting her wrists. There were blood drippings visible, a trail through the entire house. By now I was hardened and felt indifferent as to whether Grete lived or died.

One morning, as we were all gathered in the dreary surroundings, I was sitting by the window when I heard a scratching on the door. There then appeared a small boy, maybe 8 years old. He asked if our name was Baltutt, and we nodded yes. He then told us that Herr Baltutt wanted Frau Gertrud Baltutt to meet him at an particular place and bring some bread spread with lard. My heart pounded with joy. Tears came into my eyes for I thought my father had been hiding somewhere all this time and was now coming home.

Quickly Edith cut three slices of bread and spread them with lard, and the two of us wrapped the bread and ran to meet him. As we approached the area the boy had told us about, there in the distance we saw a group of men at work. We walked closer and discovered that the men were working with heavy picks and shovels to fill in the potholes in the streets that had been caused by the heavy tanks and trucks They were not alone, for with them were two Russian guards armed with machine guns.

As I searched for my father's face, I heard him calling our names, and following the direction of the sound I found my dear father. His face was pale and his eyes had sunken in his head. His clothes were dirty and his shoes were worn and likewise covered with dirt. He turned to the guard and as he spoke to him the guard nodded his head in permission.

Edith and I came and stood next to him, but were warned by the guard that we were not to touch hands or have any kind of bodily contact. My father's first words to us were, "Why didn't your mother come with you?" When we told him that she never returned that day that they had both left together, tears came into his eyes. When I saw him in pain, I wanted to hug him and tell him not to worry, that we would live, that we were taking care of our little sisters. Then he turned to the guard and told him that our mother was not with us and in desperation he asked the guard if he had seen her. My father took a picture of my mother from the inside of his coat and showed it to the guard. The guard nodded his head yes, and reported to my father that a woman that looked just like the one in the picture was working as a cook for the Russian troops.

My father looked straight into the guard's face with tears rolling down his face. He knew that the guard lied to him out of pity. Seeing us standing there without our mother and our father, the guard must have felt the agony my father felt and tried to put his mind at ease by saying he had seen her, which would mean to my father that she was alive.

I wanted so to hold his hand. I wanted to ask if I could go with him, wherever it may be. Most of all I hurt inside as I looked into his tearful eyes, his expression of despair.

My father told us that he loved us and that he would never forget us as long as he was able to breathe the breath of life. The last thing he said was that we would be together some day. Finally, the guard motioned for us to leave. My poor father, with his head bowed, turned his back to us, resting his hands on his heavy pick, waited for us

97

to move out of sight.

As we left this awful scene, I thought of the Polish prisoners I had seen in my hometown of Osterode as they walked guarded by the German SS troops. I had felt such pain for them when I looked into their empty faces. They had no future and no hope, and now our father had to partake of that same agony. I told Edith that every day we would search the city to find our father again, and maybe luck would have it, that he would be set free.

And so we did. Every day we went to search for him, but no matter how long we searched we never saw him again.

Chapter 18

Our searches for our parents were also expeditions in search of food. Herr Klein had continued to help himself to our meager food supply, and now we were always hungry. Edith and I searched in many empty houses for food, but what we found was mostly litter.

We knew that most German people kept home-canned foods in cellars on wooden shelves, so we searched in burned-out homes, found our way into the cellars, which were always dark and flooded with water, sometimes up to our waists. We could feel alongside the walls until we found wooden shelves. Then we would feel in the darkness if there were any intact jars of fruits and vegetables.

Since these shelves were frequently higher than either of us were tall, Edith would stand to her waist in the water and I would climb up on her shoulders. With one hand I would hold onto the shelves and the other hand I would pass whatever jars I found down to her. We would take as many as we could eat and share with our little sisters, then go back the next day for more. Burned houses were the best places to find food for most people shunned away from them for fear that they were not safe to walk into.

We did not know how to bake bread and therefore had to acquire bread in some other way. In our daily

99

wanderings, always searching for food, we came upon a Russian bakery where they distributed bread for the army. Knocking on the window we got the attention of a Russian. He asked us what we wanted and I, being the more sickly looking of us, asked him in Russian (by now we had picked up some basics) to please give me some bread. As usual, the Russians were always friendly towards children, and he gave us one of their loaves. Happily we hurried home to spread it with lard and share it with our little sisters.

One day, we came upon a large hospital building. The structure had been well burned and looked deserted. Edith and I searched all over for food, but found only paper bags containing powdered pea soup. We opened the paper bag and poured the powder into our palms to eat. As was our usual practice, we searched for and found the cellar of the building, and there we came upon a large ring of cheese. The ring was too heavy for us to carry and had to be rolled like a wheel. This would not do! We decided to hide the big cheese and run home to fetch the baby carriage, then come back and wheel it home.

When we arrived back at the hospital building, we found it as we left it. Edith and I could barely comprehend finding such a treasure! The cheese could last us a whole year or more, we thought. It wouldn't spoil. We lifted the big wheel of cheese into the baby carriage and pushed the carriage out of the building. The carriage was heavily weighted down with the cheese. Looking at our treasure, thinking as soon as we arrived home we would slice off pieces and eat it with the bread, we pushed the carriage towards home. Along the way a Russian truck passed us by and some of the soldiers waved to us, calling out "Privet malen'kiye devochki!"[10] meaning "Hi little girls!"

But suddenly, the truck came to a halt. Several

---

[10] Привет маленькие девочки!

soldiers got out and asked if we wanted to trade the big cheese for all the bread our carriage could hold. Before we had the chance to negotiate the trade, two of the soldiers came with their arms loaded with bread, took our cheese and filled the carriage with bread. They jumped back into the truck and waived their arms good-bye to us. When we arrived home, there was bread for everyone.

By now, Edith and I had made it a practice to go out every day and search generally everywhere. Once we came upon a bank and walked into it, finding on the floor of the bank German Marks laying all around: 10, 20, and 100 Mark bills – like a carpet of currency. Since the money was now only paper, we walked away without a second thought.

With all the snow melted by now, our main concern became the need to obtain water. In our wanderings we came upon the water company of Prussian Holland. Walking into the old grey stone building we noticed the water flowed in a constant stream down the brown, iron coated walls which fell into a concrete bed and the water level never changed. From there it flowed into a crystal clear creek-like stream bed. The big structure smelled foul of iron and other minerals, but the water looked deliciously clean and clear. Edith and I cupped our hands and drank from the water until we stilled our thirst. We needed to bring some home to our little sisters, had nothing to carry it in.

The next day we had acquired a pede. This is a device which fits over the shoulders, is usually made from wood, and has a hook and chain on each side to attach a pail. Each day, we walked across a big meadow to obtain the precious water. Edith and I had to take turns carrying the pails. When it became my turn, I felt as if I would break down under the weight of the more than half-filled pails on each side of me. I tumbled from one side to the other. My

101

feet would move by my own determination to set one foot in front of the other until it was again Edith's turn to carry the water for a stretch.

The trips to carry home the water had become a daily chore. It was now the month of March and we had given up hope of finding our parents. We knew now that they both had been kept as prisoners and were lost to us. It felt like spring outside. The birds started to chirp their sweet melodies and the grass took on a rich green color. The first flowers peeked through the black rich soil and the beautiful lilies of the valley gave off a rich smell of hope. Nothing had changed in nature. Everything just continued on, as if nothing ever happened. I felt that I, too, must follow my nature and continue to carry on.

One day I had gone to get water without Edith, and as I walked under the heavy load of my precious water, in the distance I heard the sound of trampling hooves. I stretched my head to see what it was that I heard. Now I could see that several riders on horseback were galloping speedily toward me. I stood in the middle of the open field and waited for the riders to pass by. As they came closer I saw that the riders were German boys. Their ages might have ranged between 14 and 16 years. In a wild motion they pulled the reins, the horses pawed their front hoofs and came to a halt. With their snorting breath making them sound like wild beasts, steam blew from their nostrils as they nervously trampled back and forth. I thought how giant and fearful they looked and that they could easily trample me as they would a worm. I was terrified.

One of the boys, grinning down at me, asked, "What's your name? And where do you live?" I answered him that my name was Rita and that I had gone for water for we needed it to drink. The boy seemed irritated with me and commanded me to speak louder, that he couldn't hear my voice. With that he kicked over the pail of water. The others boys laughed out loud and kicked over the other pail, which had been less than half full. It spilled out on the grass. They spurred their horses, laughing out loud, and galloped off as fast as the horses would take them. My inner self warned that I must fear that gang of boys. I felt that if I fell into their hands I would be in danger.

Our food supply had reached the point that all we had left was lard and some bread which had started to mildew. It was becoming harder to obtain food. Herr Klein was still with us and he made it understood that all the food we brought into the house had to be shared with him. Edith, not being in agreement with him, told him otherwise. Herr Klein showed his Prussian temper, and this time he lifted his cane and with it he struck Edith across the back. Edith and I had now developed an extreme dislike for Herr Klein and Edith had vowed that she would pay him back, sooner or later.

We were still fighting the lice. We tried keep our clothes and hair free of lice, but this had become impossible. Irmgard's head was now overrun with lice and we decided that her hair had to come off to give her scalp a chance to heal. With long scissors we cut back her dark hair as short as possible and with my father's razor we carefully shaved her head until she was completely bald.

Edith assured her small sister that now she was free of head lice. Irmgard looked at herself in the mirror and saw her pretty baby face marked by her deep dimples and laughed out loud. But then her deep blue eyes went serious and big tears rolled down her face. She said that she might be freed of the lice, but she was now very different from other people. She had no hair.

The lice were very bothersome at night, to the point where it seemed impossible to sleep. Since the day our parents had disappeared we had developed the habit of sleeping with our clothes on, never removing them whether it was day or night, not realizing that in so doing we had been giving the body lice more of an opportunity to breed. So no matter how often we searched the seams of our clothes to rid ourselves of the pests, it wasn't possible to be free of them.

Once again, Edith and I went back to the big hospital building, hoping to find another wheel of cheese. When we walked into the big structure, it felt hollow and empty. Searching below the main floor of the hospital we found nothing but powdered pea soup scattered about. I took an envelope of the pea soup and walked upstairs where there was light; Edith was exploring elsewhere. Sitting on the floor I poured out the powder into my hands and ate it out of my palms. Then I heard footsteps. I sat still and listened. They came closer. Then a man appeared in view. Unlike the familiar sight of the Russians in uniform this man wore civilian clothes. He was well dressed, wearing a trench coat and a hat. I did not know what he wanted of me when he walked over to me. He asked, "What are you doing alone in this building?" I answered that I was hungry and was looking for food.

The man spoke in German with a heavy accent. He asked if I also needed shoes and clothes and I nodded my head. With that he lifted me up and sat me on a table. He then touched my dress and said that he would see to it that I would have a new dress. He then took my leg lifted it and asked what size shoes I might wear. Again I told him that I did not know. When he lifted my dress up and asked if I needed underwear I became afraid. It was as if the Lord spoke to me, telling me whom to trust and whom to me afraid of. Sitting on the table I knew I had to get away.

When the man turned to look around to find something to take the measurements of my foot I jumped off the table and ran as fast as my legs could run, all the while yelling for Edith to run from the man. I did not realize that by that time the Polish forces were in the process of taking

104

over a part of the East Prussian territory and that the man had been of the Polish occupying forces.

At the Yalta conference, decisions were made to transfer the northern portion of East Prussia, including Königsberg, now Kaliningrad, to the U.S.S.R. and the territories east of a line extending from the Czechoslovakian frontier along the Meise River to the Oder River and the Baltic Sea were allocated to Poland. Now there were many Poles and Russians in the lands of what was now the former East Prussia.

Everyday homes were still in flames. The Russian soldiers had made it a practice to celebrate the end of the war. They drank Vodka, raped women – and to have a really good time, they poured gasoline into the hallway of houses, threw a match on it and the house would then burn down to the ground, never giving a thought whether the house was occupied or not.

We had become friends with two young Russian soldiers. At first they loved to pay attention to my two little sisters, Irmgard and Waltraut. They liked to play with them by sitting them up on their knees and singing to them.

In our bedroom they kept their musical instrument, an accordion, which we had to hide under blankets from some other soldiers, if they found it, they would surely take it away. Their names were Loshka and Zoshka, and they belonged to one of the tank outfits. They were both very young, maybe just 18 or 19 years old.

The two would come often. They taught us to speak Russian and taught us their songs. We became very befriended by them. We asked Loshka and Zashka where we could obtain food for we had no bread at all. They told us that if we went to the Russian field kitchen that we might be able to find work, which would be paid for in food. The very next day Edith and I walked to the kitchen carrying a container for the food we might be given.

Chapter 19

It was a large building where warm food was prepared for the Russian troops. Edith and I walked to the window for we were never allowed inside. As we asked if they could spare some Kasha for my sisters and ourselves, they told us that if we wanted food we had to work to earn it. They showed us to a courtyard of the building and there they told us we could come and peel potatoes. As payment at the end of the day, we could earn a container with Kasha (grits).

In the courtyard, there stood a bathtub type container which had to be filled each day with potatoes. Several old German women were seated on stools around the big tub and peeling away, not even looking up at us children. A young Russian soldier brought stools and gave us a knives. Edith and I were content to sit until early evening and peel the potatoes for the next day. At the end of the day together with the older women we walked to the kitchen window and each received two ladles of Kasha, which we carried home and shared with our little sisters. Seeing this as a steady source of food, we returned on succeeding days to peel potatoes.

One day as we peeled the potatoes, the young soldier came to talk to Edith and me. He started to sing a few of his songs to us and we tried to make conversation. He laughed with us when we tried to explain using half Russian and half German words.

At one point, I jokingly lifted his army hat off his head and threw it on the ground. I could not believe the transformation which took place in the once pleasant soldier. Angrily, he stood up and with flashing angry eyes he shouted words at me. He then pointed to the Soviet Red Star on his hat, put his hat back on his head and ordered that I must leave and that I could not come there again. I then realized that I had insulted not the person, but that I had shown disrespect for the Russian Star, the red symbol of the Soviet Union. I then remembered that I had done the same as my mother had done when she called the German officer in uniform a cripple.

Around this time it occurred to me that we had not seen or heard from Grete in many weeks. I often wondered what might have happened to her. She could have been taken by the Russians, just like my parents, or – it crossed my mind that she might also have succeeded in taking her life after all.

Walking across an empty field, the sun warmed my frail body. Deep in thought, thinking of my parents that I had lost, I could see them both before me in my mind. The memory of my father's face, twisting in agony as he said, "Someday we will be together again," brought tears into my eyes. In my mind, I tried to implant a better memory of him. I thought about my home in Osterode. I thought of him as he lifted me up off the floor, when he gave me the rollerscooter and said, "It has been a joy making the scooter for you." With that, he had sat me down on the scooter with a smile on his face. I thought to myself, this is the memory I want to keep of him. I thought of my mother; could she not be at least with us? Why did they take both? How will we live? Waltraut is only four and Irmgard six years old. We have very little water, scarcely enough to drink. There is no electricity, no food, there are no stores, and the money is laying all over the bank for people to step on. There is no hospital if we become ill or need medicine. The lice will eat us alive if we can't wash and have clean clothes.

As I walked along the open field, I came upon a figure laying in a ditch. A German soldier with his arms stretched out, his face turned to one side. I looked upon him thinking, no one but me knows where his body is. His family will search for him some day not knowing whether he is dead or alive. The flies were crawling in and out of the cavity of his eyes and nose. I thought, if I had a piece of cloth I would cover his head, and I walked away.

Walking to our quarters, my two little sisters were sitting on the window bench looking down at the Russian trucks riding back and forth on our street. Herr Klein, as always, was resting in the big chair, his cane within reach, smoking his daily cigar that he so enjoyed – well hidden under the chifferobe there a wooden box filled with the best brand of cigars.

When I asked for Edith, he raised himself out of the chair and angrily reported that he had to teach her a lesson with his cane and that she had left. I had never talked back to Herr Klein because I feared him and also hated his proud character. I sat huddled on the window bench sitting with my two little sisters. I tried to look down the street in hopes that I might see a glimpse of Edith. We needed each other, for it took the two of us working together every day to search for our daily bread.

It was not long before the big sliding door which separated the living room from the bedroom, was suddenly opened by someone. There in the doorway stood a Russian soldier in full uniform, armed with a submachine gun. Standing there a few seconds, he looked around, seeing the old man sitting in the big chair by the stove, the soldier asked if his name was Klein. The old man jumped to his feet, grabbed his cane, and nodded yes.

With that, the soldier walked straight to the chifferobe, and like he knew exactly where to find them, grabbed the box of cigars. He opened the box to see that it was the thing he was after, smelled one of them and shut the lid. Herr Klein stood in disbelief with his hand stretched out, and begged the soldier to leave him just one. "Just one," he begged again. The soldier ignored him and turned on his heel and left with the cigars as quickly as he had come.

Herr Klein was now furious, knew that Edith had taken revenge, and threatened that he would punish her. She had arranged to take away the only enjoyment he had left in the darkness of his existence – he had no further words for such an outrage but settled back into his chair, probably to darkly reflect upon the misery of his life without food and now without his daily cigar.

The next morning, a small boy came to the house telling me to come with him, that my sister Edith, wanted to see me. I followed him until walking through a small alley, we came upon a stretch of small red brick houses. The alley smelled of motor oil and foul garbage. "Here it is," the boy said, pointing out a door. I opened the door and walked in. Here I found my sister, Edith, sitting on the bed. With her was another girl, somewhat older, maybe 12 years old. She had dark hair and her name was Erika.

With a smile of triumph, Edith asked what the face of Herr Klein looked like when he lost his precious cigars to the Soviet army. With that, we all broke out in laughter, especially Edith. She was proud of how she had retaliated. Edith then told me that it was not all she had in mind and that she would come back to stay and would also make sure that Herr Klein would never hit her with his cane again.

When I asked what else she had in mind, she told me

that she was going to go to the Russian Headquarters and state her complaint. She will tell them that we have already lost our parents and that Herr Klein cannot separate her from the family we have left. I suggested to Edith that they might not care to listen to her complaint and just send her away, that we should find another roof over our heads and forget about Herr Klein. But Edith would not hear of it. She explained that if there was ever a chance for our parents to be set free, they would look for us in that very house where we were last together. I agreed that this was so. I asked Edith if she had food? She then told me the soldier had given her and Erika bread for in exchange for the information about the cigars.

The little flat that Edith and Erika shared looked depressing. There was no order, the place had been looted, pieces of furniture had been broken, there was glass laying all around, and the bed consisted of a rumpled mass of dirty bed clothes in a messy pile. I was lost without Edith and wanted her with us. I had hoped that she would come back with me that very minute, but she insisted upon staying away.

Herr Klein, now always in a bad frame of mind over the loss of his good cigars, never had a kind word for us children, not that he had much to say to us before. He told us to just stay out of his way, but he never told us to go away for he knew that with us little children there, he was somewhat protected from the Russians.

Finally the day I was waiting for arrived – Edith came home. Edith entered the room accompanied by a Russian officer who held her by the hand. The officer confronted Herr Klein, who had gotten out of his chair and stood erect facing both the officer and Edith. The officer then asked the old man in German how old he was? If it were true what the girl had reported. Herr Klein wanted to report that Edith had been unruly, but he was interrupted by the

Russian, who ordered him to report every day at daybreak to a place where he would be given work taking into consideration his age and disability, which was a crippled leg. He further ordered him to inflict no harm to any of us and told him that we children had the right to stay together and could not be separated. After writing down Herr Klein's name, he ordered him to be at the specified location in the morning. The officer then promptly left.

Herr Klein never tried to discipline Edith again, but left each morning to return at night.

Edith now had the upper hand over us and became our substitute mother. She was eleven years old.

It was now the middle of May, with the trees starting to bud and bloom in every color of the rainbow. The sun with its warmth gave us hope. Edith and I continued to explore the ruins to find ways into cellars where could search for home canned foods. The task was still very unpleasant, for we had to stand in cold water up to our waists and in the darkness, searching to find jars of food which we more often could not find.

Also, we still carried water from the town's water company, always worrying about meeting with that gang of German teenagers I so feared. I had learned to walk close to shrubs and trees so I could quickly hide.

Chapter 20

Loshka and Zashka often came to use our house to drink their vodka and sing their songs and laugh. They never brought food, for I think they had very little themselves. I always worried that in their drunkenness they might pour gasoline into our hallway and burn us all to death.

`One evening, Loshka and Zashka had come to spend their free time at our house, talking loud and rowdy. They were already drunk with vodka. Loshka tumbled into our quarters in his full tank uniform, wearing his large quilted hat with the red star of Russia in the center, and he looked fierce. Pulling out a large bottle of vodka, he told his friend to sit and drink with him. Zashka happily pulled out a metal cup from under his jacket and motioned him to fill it up.

As they started to drink, it became obvious that they had had more than enough. They started to sing very loudly, but their tongues were heavy and they only blurted out some incoherent melody. Talking with each other, they laughed and filled their cups with vodka again and again. Zashka, tried to get up from the chair, but just tumbled back and sat down again. It became quiet. I thought perhaps they were so intoxicated that sleep would follow.

Suddenly, Loshka, looked up at me with a dazed expression, and asked, "Where is Edith?" Edith sitting in the corner of the darkened room, silently crawled under the bed. She knew that in their state she could not trust them. I told him that I didn't know where she was. But now he yelled louder and demanded Edith. By now I had become frightened and again told him that I did not know where she could be. Edith, also frightened, did not move in her hiding place. Loshka then told his friend to come help him search for her.

Yelling her name as loud as possible, Zashka staggered out of the bedroom into the hallway of the house. Loshka held his machine gun up into the air, yelling for Edith. Knowing they were not in their right mind and dazed with drunkenness, I shivered with fear. Still holding the machine gun with one hand and holding on to the banister of the stairway with the other, Loshka yelled some profanities and rattled his bullets into the ceiling of the bedroom. I started to scream with terror, the sound of the machine gun was as if the worst bolt of lightning had struck us. The ceiling split and plaster came falling down on us in big chunks.

With this, Loshka and Zashka made it down the stairs and staggered out of the house. Edith still hid under the bed, and I heard my voice still screaming. "We have to leave this place; the house might fall in on us any moment," I yelled. My two small sisters also sobbed with fright. As I ran out to make sure the drunken soldiers had left, I told Edith to come out of her hiding place and prepare to get out of this house of horrors.

Edith now appeared, and she, too, was crying because of the terrible thing, agreed and said we would leave right away. I told Edith that we must not underestimate their anger and that they might pour gasoline into the hallway like their comrades had done many times to other houses and we might parish in the flames.

That night, we made a bed in a dark corner of the entrance to the house, huddled together and waited until morning.

The next morning we gathered our meager belongings, which consisted of a small amount of lard and left the last place where we once lived together with our parents. Our ties were now severed. If one or both ever returned, we could not be found. With that, we also detached ourselves from the tyrant Herr Klein.

Looking for shelter was not as hard as searching for food. We concluded that it would be safer to live on a street which was lined with houses. There, we could pick a house in the center of the street and not many Russians would come upon us too often. So it was, we found a small house. Making it livable, we cleaned it of the rubble and garbage which had been thrown around by the looting soldiers. Edith and I set up beds for the four of us and we made it our next home. Our quarters consisted of a bedroom and a kitchen. It was warmer now and we had no need to fire a stove, which stood always in the main room. Now all we needed was food to eat. Edith gave instructions to Irmgard and Waltraut never to wander off, but to stay in or around our new home. We never included them when we went out on our scavenging expeditions.

The day after we settled into our new home, we located a nearby farm and visited to observe what was going on. Many women were busy working in the field, and some tended to milk cows. We sat down among a patch of cucumbers, and to my amazement, there before my eyes were young cucumbers that we could just pick and eat, as many as we wanted! The cucumbers tasted very good without having to peel off the skin for they were young and tender.

Soon a Polish woman shouted to us that we were not

to eat their cucumbers and we left the patch to walk toward the field in which the cows were milked. There, an apparatus was set up, a centrifuge which separated the cream from the milk. A Polish woman was operating it, and it was clear they were all Poles. Looking at me she said, "If you bring a container, we will give you all the skimmed milk that you can carry."

From that day on, we carried home skim milk. When it soured and became thick, we could then eat it with a spoon. I remember that every day we could drink and also eat the soured milk as much as we wanted. Now, instead of carrying water, we carried home milk, which became our life-sustaining food for as long as we remained in Prussian Holland, East Prussia.

It seemed as though no German people were to be found on farms. All the farms were occupied by Poles, mostly women. The women worked in the fields and did all the chores.

I have imprinted in my mind that the Poles were the cruelest human beings I have ever encountered in my young life. Their hatred for the Germans was so strong that they had no mercy. They did not ask if the Germans were Bolsheviks, but killed them in cold blood. They drove the Germans away from their farms by shooting them and taking their infants by the neck, throwing them against the wall, then claimed the land. Unlike the Russians, the Polish soldiers had no compassion for any German, whether infant or adult. Whenever we spotted a Polish soldier, we knew well to find a hiding place.

The warmth of the early summer had brought with it flies and bed bugs, and together with the body lice and head lice, the lack of water for bathing. Diseases like cholera and typhoid broke out. The dead were wrapped in sheets and dumped into holes in the ground. Looking at the dead, stiff bodies wrapped in sheets, I thought of having to do the same with one of us if death occurred to me or one of my sisters. The flies covered white walls in some places like a black blanket of death.

In my adult life many times I searched for the answer of why disease did not befall one of us. We too had suffered hunger, lack of cleanliness, were surrounded by flies, and suffered from lice. I concluded that the sour milk must have been the factor keeping us disease free. The sour milk might have contained a substance to make our body immune to even a common cold.

The wheat and rye of the Polish farmers stood waving in the wind, like a lake of gold waiting to be harvested. In a potato field I saw many women, among them, some German nuns weeding the field. My eyes were drawn to the sight of a woman sitting in the middle of the field; she waved her head and arms in a continuous motion. Her hair was dark and in disarray. Her entire body shook with a never ending jerk. She sat dressed in a white robe and had bare feet.

Looking at the German nuns, I assumed they might be caring for her. I had never seen anything that helpless and pitiful. Walking over to the sick woman to observe her closer, I asked the nun what might be wrong with her. She explained that she was suffering from an affliction called St. Vitus Dance.

A while later, the sick woman stood up and walked across the field with her arms twitching and her face twisted in a grimace. The nuns took no notice as she walked away. I asked Edith if we should follow her to see what she was up to.

As we slowly followed the sick woman, more young children followed who also were curious to see where a woman in such a condition would walk to. Suddenly, appearing like the devil out of nowhere, came the gang of German teenage boys with whom I had an unfavorable experience.

116

This time they had no horses; there were four of them. One carried a shovel in his hand and another carried a pitchfork. They started to mimic the woman. Teasing her, they pushed her from one side to the other until she fell. As she stood up again, it was apparent that the woman was naked underneath her robe; with nothing but a rope tied around her waist. The gang now burst out with loud laughter, and pushed her again to get her to fall. The poor woman all the while mumbled incoherent sounds and twisted her face in ugly grimaces. One of the boys then pushed her into an empty house.

As I stood there feeling sorry for the unfortunate sick woman, I wished so that I could help her and bring her back to the nuns in the potato field, but I really did not want to be burdened with her.

There was no law one could call upon. The whole country was in a chaotic state. Everyone tried to survive on their own. One could live in any house they pleased. There was no debt to pay, no rent to pay, there were no stores, and there was lawlessness.

Now, the woman appeared in the doorway. She was completely naked with only the rope tied around her waist. The boys roared with laughter. Edith and I should have left the scene but we did not.

Naked as she was, the gang of boys pushed her to walk forward. I don't believe the woman could understand what was happening to her. Her face was so twisted that one could not guess her age with any accuracy. From her body, I could tell she must have been in her twenties or early thirties. The boys pushed her to walk onto a field and stopped by a narrow creek in which the water flowed crystal clear. The water in the creek was about 2 feet deep. There, they pushed the poor woman until she fell face down into the water. Every time she climbed back up to the grass, the wild gang pushed her back in again. She made many attempts to climb back out, but was repeatedly pushed into the water. As she struggled to climb out for the last time, one of the teenage boys took his pitchfork and held her head under the water. I could see the bubbles emerging to the surface. My stomach muscles started to contract and I wanted to vomit. I ran from the scene trying to hold down the sick feeling I had. My last encounter with the teenage boys left in me the fear of horses, which are to man the most useful and gentle of all animals. Now they left me in fear for my life.

Chapter 21

On a warm afternoon, together with Edith and our friend Erika exploring the area in which we now lived in back of a house in a wild garden, overgrown with weeds, had found a swing tied with ropes from an oak tree. Happily, we spent some time taking turns on the swing, singing songs at play, and talking loudly with each other. Suddenly, we heard the trampling of horses. As I turned my head toward the sound, I noticed that the boys had already spotted us and were riding toward us. As we ran from them, they sped up their horses and were right on our heels again, laughing devilishly.

We ran into an entrance of a vacant house. The three of us were crying out loud with fright. One of the hoodlum boys jumped off his horse and came running after us; grabbing Erika by the neck. I was so terrified that I could not think of what to do. I ran up a flight of stairs to the attic and hid under the rafters of the roof. Another boy now had my sister Edith. They were still searching for me and as I laid there between the planks of the roof, I could hear my heart beat. I tried not to breathe and tried to snuggle like a worm under the planks which I thought could hide me from their sight. I heard the footsteps of the boy come closer, and I dared not to look. Now, he had spotted me. It was no use, I could not get away.

I was very much aware of their cruelty and knew that any moment now we would be trampled to death by their horses. Shivering from fear and pleading with the boy to set me free, he showed a spark of emotion when he told me that when my turn came to crawl under the bellies of their horses, I must be careful not to touch their skins for the sensation could make them kick at me.

Standing before them with tears streaming down my face, I cried uncontrollably. The horses were hot-blooded race horses. Their eyes looked big and wild at me, and their movement was constant. Their hoofs tapped on the ground as if they were ready to speed away. Now the leader of the gang told us for punishment, we would have to crawl under the bellies of their horses, one by one. He pointed at Edith and said that she was first. I had managed to whisper to her and Erika not to touch their bellies. I can't quite remember how I made it when my turn came to crawl beneath their bellies, but all of us made it. With red faces, now crying for joy, we were saved.

All my life since then, I have never sat on a horse or even dared to touch one for I know that they surely would feel the fear I have of them and perhaps hurt me.

Summer turned to fall, it was September, and I turned nine years old. Russian troops started moving slowly out of Prussian Holland, and the Poles with their families started moving in. Prussian Holland now had a new name: Pasłęk. And according to those agreements between the Allied nations, it came time for the remaining Germans to be deported to Berlin.

By now, my sisters and I had starved to the point that we had no meat on our bones but only skin which covered our skeletons. Especially me. More than ever before I looked like I was suffering from starvation. From birth I had had a weak appearance, with a tiny-boned build, small faced with white blond hair. My cheeks had now fallen in, which really emphasized my big, piercing, blue eyes. My arms and legs had shriveled as if they were made of sticks. My stomach did not protrude, but looked hollow beneath my rib cage. My hip bones were covered with thin skin and stuck out from my lower torso.

Our food now consisted of sour milk and granules of wheat or rye we could find in the fields and apples from apple trees that the summer had blessed us with. Bread had become a luxury and continued to be a luxury for years to come, even after returning to Germany.

All the while, after we had severed our ties with Herr Klein, we had never had any contact or conversation with adults, until one day we received a visitor. An old, grey-headed lady walked into our little room. She introduced herself with the name Frau Pavendenat. She explained to us that she had noticed our movements and assumed we had lost our parents to the Russians. In a motherly way, she told us of a transport which had been set up by the Poles for the Germans remaining in the area to evacuate to Berlin. She said it would be good for us to get on the train, for there they would take care of orphans like us. She also told us that in Berlin there was order. They had water which flowed out of the faucet, electricity, and the German mark actually had some value. She then told us that if we neglected to get on the train, we most likely would remain in East Prussia to grow up to become Polish citizens some day.

Edith and I listened to the old woman with great intensity. She had been sent to us like an angel from heaven, and a good thing, too, because we knew nothing of this evacuation train. She promised that she would be back by next morning and would provide us with a loaf of bread for our journey. Irmgard and Waltraut were only 4 and 6 years old, too young to comprehend what would happen the very next day. But many years later, when I told her about this event, Waltraut remembered something I had forgotten. Frau Pavendenat had also provided us with a large bag of cooked lima beans to eat on our journey. This was something that she had remembered rather fondly.

Edith and I were overjoyed with great expectation. We waited in great impatience until the morning arrived. In preparation for the trip we gathered some blankets with which to keep warm on the train, but we had nothing else but the insect-infested clothing we wore on our thin bodies. We did not even have a picture of our parents or anything to remind us of our home to take with us.

The next morning, Frau Pavendenat came back as promised. Wrapped in a cloth, she handed to us a loaf of rye bread which might have weighed 4 pounds, and the beans. She gave her last advice to Edith and with a soft, but worried look in her eyes, she said, "You must make this bread last until you arrive in Berlin. It may take weeks before you get to your destination; therefore, have one slice of bread each day and no more."

We asked her if she was not going to go on the train with us, but she replied that she planned to remain here where her husband was buried, so that she could be buried with him in the end. In any event, she said she was too old to start life anew elsewhere and didn't mind becoming a Polish citizen.

Frau Pavendenat accompanied us to the train, told us good-by and good luck, turned around and left. She did not go with us but only showed us the way. It was midday. The freight train looked so very long that I could not see the end of the last car.

In front of each box car were bundles stacked up, 2 to 3 feet high. The Polish authorities had announced that all people were to leave their belongings behind and the only baggage they could bring with them were the necessities to sustain life, which consisted of the clothing they wore, their food, and a container for their daily functions. This time

there was no straw for warmth, the floor was bare. Edith and I spread out our blankets and we settled ourselves close to the big sliding door of the car. We placed our bread underneath our blankets and guarded our food constantly.

Finally, everyone seemed to be settled, and few people spoke with each other. Our car seemed to be filled with young women and their small children, and elderly people with their spouses. There was no-one of our parents ages. Looking outside the train, I could see the Polish military guards armed with their guns and other Polish officials in civilian clothes going in and out of cars.

Three of the civilian officials climbed into our car. They asked if everyone had understood to leave personal belongings by the car on the sidewalk and the people that had not been made aware of the rule should obey it now.

They started to check through the people in the car to see if they had observed the rule; all the while, one of the officials constantly looked at me.

They started to spot check several people for they had also announced that it is forbidden to take with them any German money. One of the officials picked out an old man, told him to stand up and open his jacket. The man opened his jacket and the Pole examined his inside pocket. From it, he pulled out several German mark bills. When he found the money in the old man's pocket, he grabbed him by the shoulder, and with his fist, hit the man in the face. The man fell amongst the other people, who now had worried looks on their faces. The Pole picked the man up again by his jacket and looking further, he pulled out a 5 x 7 picture of a young German soldier.

He bellowed at the man, asking who it was in the picture. He answered that it was the picture of his dead son and begged to keep it. With that, the angered Pole hit him in the face over and over until blood spurted out of his nose and mouth. After he was knocked down again, the man still pleaded to let him have the only memento of his son he had left. Again, the Pole grabbed the man, tearing his cloth. In his pants pocket, he found a bag of tobacco. He took the bag, tore it open, and threw the contents of the bag over the old man's head. He then tore the picture of his son into little pieces and discarded the pieces to blow in the wind. The old man just laid on the floor weeping and trying not to move.

His next victim was an old lady sitting on the floor. He commanded her to stand up. When she answered that she could not stand without her crutches, which stood leaning against the wall, the Pole pulled the old woman up by her coat; checked her pockets and with a heavy push, he threw her back down while she yelped in pain.

As I sat huddled together with my sisters, I felt the same sick feeling in my stomach that I felt that day the German hoodlums had drowned the sick, naked woman in the creek. The officials were finally done with our railcar. Still staring at the miserable scene, I felt something in the palm of my hand. When I shifted my eyes to see what it was I was holding, I looked into the face of the Polish official who had been staring at me earlier. Putting his finger in front of his lips, he signaled that I must keep quiet, and then left with his fellows. As we examined what it was I had in my hand, Edith and I counted 500 German marks.

Silently, I buried the money together with the bread under my blanket. Evening had begun, but we were still sitting on the tracks. Babies and little children had become restless and were beginning to cry from the discomfort of the freight car. But then finally the train started to roll out of the station. As it did, my sisters and I had our first slice of bread from Frau Pavendenat's loaf, as we left our precious homeland, East Prussia, which had now become Poland.

Next to us stood a baby buggy, holding an infant who was six weeks old. It cried continuously. The young mother tried to cuddle the baby, quietly praying over him

124

that he might survive until they reached Berlin. She could not breastfeed the baby for she had no nourishment. Chewing up some bread, she tried feed it to the baby from her mouth.

The train rolled on for a few hours. The trip was never a continuous ride, but the train traveled for only a few hours each day. Sometimes it would move no more than one or two hours and then stop for many hours more. These stops sometimes lasted a full day. The road distance from Prussian Holland, East Prussia to Berlin is approximately 600 kilometers, and with all the stop and go it did indeed take a couple of weeks to arrive in Berlin.

Lice and disease accompanied all of us on the trip and some people came down with cholera — the disease had spread all through the entire train. And some died. The dead were not kept in the railcar, but were always dumped when the train was in motion. Every day, one or two people died and they were always disposed of in the same manner. No one took note of their identification. Most people had no next of kin and no home address. I suppose anyone of us four sisters could have died from cholera in that car, but in my child's mind, it never occurred to me that it could strike me. I always somehow knew it would be others who would die, but never me.

On one of our extended stops, Edith and I left the train to roam, but not too far from it. We came upon another train, this time a passenger train on a parallel set of tracks. The Russian soldiers on the train were gaily shouting and waving their arms at us. By now, I had learned that my pathetic appearance and the starved look in my face could pay off in food. Also, I knew that the Russians liked children.

I walked up to the train with my hands stretched up toward the window with many heads looking down at me, I asked for *kleba* (bread). Some of the soldiers threw chunks of bread down at me and one of them gave me a container of warm noodle soup. The noodle soup was so precious to me for it had been the first warm food I had tasted in many months.

This is a moment in my life I will cherish. The simple food of noodle soup was utter happiness for me. And in spite of the loss of my precious parents, I never developed a dislike for the Russians. I found them to be warm and good-hearted people.

We had spent many days on the freight train. The young mother was still desperately trying to keep her infant alive until we reached our destination. The baby in the buggy looked frail and starved. His face looked very unlike the babies I know now. His face was long and his cheeks fallen in. On one occasion, the young mother had him checked by another passenger to see if he was still alive.

The passenger, a woman, told the mother it would not be long now. Using a superstitious phrase, she said, "He is raising his arms to heaven, it won't be long before he is dead." His worried mother hovered over him constantly. She kept feeding him chewed up bread and cuddled him in her arms.

We were now approaching the river Oder that divided East Germany from Poland. The people in the car were now saying that we were not far from Berlin and should arrive there within a day if the train would just keep moving at the same rate.

Just after crossing into Germany, in the morning hours of the twelfth day, the train once more came to a halt. The big door came open; outside it was dark and cold I heard the voices of many German men asking us to please make room for some wounded veterans who would be riding with us to Berlin.

In the semi-darkness, I could see the pitiful,

unshaven faces of my countrymen. Many had crutches, some had lost an arm or a leg. Their clothes were torn and all German military insignia had been removed. Many had no shoes and their feet were wrapped instead with canvas. Some moaned in pain. My heart ached for them and I could not resist thinking of my father. His face had looked broken, just like the faces of these defeated German soldiers. Searching all their faces carefully, I was hoping to find, maybe by chance, the face of my father.

Part Three: East Berlin

Chapter 22

After fourteen days of misery, the huge freight train with 30,000 deported Germans from East Prussia arrived in the morning of November 1945 at the Lehrter Train Station of Berlin. Awaiting the train were many nurses working for the Red Cross and other personnel with badges marked "Red Cross." The young mother with the sick, starved baby was been taken care of immediately. The baby was taken from her by a nurse and they were rushed immediately to a hospital. Other sick people with cholera and typhoid were placed into ambulances and were likewise carried off to a hospital.

One Red Cross nurse then called out that all parentless children should come forward. Edith and I, together with Irmgard and Waltraut, gathered around the nurse. She stood in the midst of us with a pad and a pencil wanting to know all the details of our birth, the names of any relatives we could remember, and their addresses, and the full names of our parents and the place of our separation. I could scarcely remember the dates of my own birthday, much less the birth dates of my parents or addresses of any relatives.

Edith promptly gave her all the information, but misstated the birthday of Irmgard by one year. Instead of being six years old, she was marked down as five. After the nurse had all the information about us, she told us to remain in our car until later that evening, when someone would take us to a shelter. For the first time, we had come to a place where I felt that people cared about us.

Edith had taken the advice of the old lady who provided us with the large loaf of bread and she had rationed it to us, only one slice a day. The day we arrived in Berlin, the only piece of bread we had left was the heel which had become quite hard, and the beans were long gone. All of us stretched our bodies and started to explore the large station.

Across from the train station was a line of barrack-type buildings. Continuing our explorations, we walked into the barracks and found that there were women there busy doing some kind of office work. They stopped work and motioned for us to come in, asking where we were from. We told them our story and how we became separated from our parents and that we had spent many days on the transport coming to Berlin. They listened with interest, and before we departed they shared with us their sandwiches, which I later found out were rationed to them in a meager supply.

Edith was going to walk back to our box car to be with our two small sisters when I told her that I would take the money the Pole had given us and try to buy food with it. When I went to collect it, I found only a portion of the money. With it, I walked across the way until I reached an exit gate. In front of the gate I found a German policeman guarding the train station. He looked at me in a friendly way and smiled. I asked him, if I had money and wanted to buy food, where could I buy some? The policeman smiled at me, and with a big grin, he said, "The only place you can buy food is at the black market." Assuming the black market was just a market like any other, I then asked how many kilometers I would have to walk to come to this black market? The policeman shrugged his shoulders and said,

"Maybe ten minutes or so."

He was a city person and did not gauge kilometers but minutes. I had no comprehension of time, and could only judge by thinking of kilometers. As I asked over and over how many kilometers it was to find the black market, he repeatedly told me it was only a ten-minute walk.

Irritated with him, I thanked him and walked out of the gate. The first place I came to was a *Bierstube*[11]. With the money in my hand, I walked into the establishment. The man behind the bar asked what I wanted. I laid twenty marks on the bar and asked for a malt beer (malt beer in Germany is a sweet drink, dark in color, with rich foam at the top of the drink – it is similar to root beer, but it doesn't taste like it at all).

As I eagerly finished my drink, the bartended counted out the change I was to receive back from buying the drink. To my amazement, in return for the one bill I had given him, he counted out many to give back to me. At that age, I had absolutely no comprehension of money and had been under the impression that everything should cost one piece of money and now he gave back to me many bills. I was overjoyed that now I had more bills then I had when I walked in.

At that age, I had only completed the second grade and had never been given the opportunity to spend money or even hold it in my hand. I gave up on the idea of finding the black market and walked back to the train.

I found Edith sitting quietly with our sisters, asked why I had not bought any bread? I explained that I had no idea how long a ten-minute walk would take to go to the black market and that the policeman at the gate refused to tell the distance in kilometers.

At late afternoon, a bus arrived. It was white with a red cross marked on each side. It was filled with other

---

[11] A small bar that sells drinks by the glass.

131

children.   A nurse stopped at our box car, got out, and read off the names of my sisters and I.   She led us to the bus and told us to be seated.   We left the blankets on the train so entered East Berlin with nothing but the clothes on our backs.   As I looked at the city, I could only see ruins. There were seemingly endless rows of bombed out houses, no matter which window I looked out of.

We stopped at a school building that had been made into a shelter.   There the nurse led us into a gymnasium whose walls were lined with bunk beds.   She assigned us to beds and told us that we would be given warm food shortly. The gymnasium was filled with many children, all of whom had suffered the same fate as we had.   Their parents had either died during the war or were taken by the Russian forces.

There were boys and girls of all ages.   The boys were spending their time grooming from lice and took no notice of us new arrivals.   We made ourselves comfortable by sitting together on the beds, watching the other children, and silently waiting for the food that was promised to us.

A woman wearing a white apron and a white scarf on her head wheeled in the cart with the food.   With a ladle, she spooned out a portion of hot steaming cereal and a slice of white bread for each child.   The cereal had been prepared with white flour and powdered milk.   It tasted slightly sweet and had the consistency of pudding.   I had not tasted anything that delicious since the day I ate the noodle soup the Russian soldiers gave me.   The food warmed my body and gave me a good feeling of being cared for.   It had been so very long since a mother's hand had cared for us and given us a clean bed to sleep in and clean clothes to wear.

For all the ten months in Prussian Holland, we had never been able to clean our hair or our bodies with soap and water.   Now, it seemed that all our hopes would become reality. On the bunks, the children found a white gown for them to sleep in. I felt I had come into a new world where there was order, warmth, and concern. Most of all, they had law enforcement. The policeman at the gate of the train station indicated that Berlin had a police force.

A Red Cross nurse entered the gymnasium. She asked for the attention of all the children with a friendly smile. She welcomed us to the East sector of Berlin and told us that the shelter we were given was temporary and that from there we could anticipate being given a new home with either adoptive parents or foster parents. Every day parents would pick out children of their choice and they would go live in a home atmosphere. When she explained that sisters and brothers would not be able to stay together, a feeling of sadness overwhelmed me for I knew it was now inevitable that soon the strong ties and concern we had developed for each other would be severed. Each of us will find a home with different people I thought, and maybe we will never see each other again.

I loved my sisters, they were a part of my life, they were my family and they were all I had left. Together we had lived to see the Russians leave and the Poles march into our homeland. Together we survived, when thousands of people died of cholera and typhoid diseases, and together we had made it to Berlin with only one slice of bread for each of us each day for fourteen days. In the freight car we had been housed like cattle and lice spread among the people even more. But together we had made it to our destination. Now, it seemed that we were going to have to part. I became worried.

When I looked at Edith, she had tears in her eyes. She gathered all of us together and told us not to be afraid, because she would remain in the gymnasium until everyone of us had been placed. She would write down their addresses and would then know where each of us would live.

Edith told us that we must not hide when people came

to look at us but that we must go with them when they asked us to. Again, Edith assured us that she would not go until she knew everyone's whereabouts. That night, for the first time in many months, dressed in my clean gown, I slept as if lying on an angel's wing.

Chapter 23

The next day, the first prospective foster parents arrived. They were mostly women but sometimes they were accompanied by men. They all initially stopped at the doorway of the large auditorium and looked at all the children. After they had someone picked out, they proceeded to walk toward them to look at them more closely, or the women paraded around the bunks on which the children were seated.

Sitting on my bunk, observing the parade, I noticed a middle-aged lady smiling at Irmgard. She stood in front of Irmgard and asked her whether she was a boy or a girl. Irmgard, with her dimpled cheeks, her large deep blue eyes, and a pretty smile answered that she was a girl and that her hair had been shaved in order to rid her of lice. The lady smiled with a warm, motherly smile and sat on the bunk next to Irmgard. She took her little hands in hers and with a warm look in her eyes, she asked, "Would you like to come home with me, and have me as your new mommy?" Irmgard answered with a smile that she would have to ask her sister Edith.

With that, the woman positioned herself to talk with all four of us, introduced herself as Frau Bach. She then asked questions about our parents and how it happened that we had lost them.

With great interest she listened with a sympathetic face, and she told us that she would like to give our sister, Irmgard, a good home. She had never had children of her own and she would do what she could to see to it that we could see each other as often as possible. Frau Bach was 47 years old.

Frau Bach made a very warm and sincere impression on Edith and I, and we felt that with her, Irmgard would be the first one of us to find a good home. So Irmgard would be the first of us to join a new family.

Edith had the address of Frau Bach, and as we said good-bye to Irmgard, Frau Bach assured us that she too would keep in touch with the Red Cross to be informed of our whereabouts. She then led Irmgard by the hand out of the door.

There were now only the three of us.

On that first day, after Irmgard was chosen, none of the rest of us were. Many of these people, as they walked around and looked at the children, seemed to look at me in particular. The blood rushed into my head every time they looked at me, but no one ever asked whether I wanted to come home with them. Edith always remained in the background observing the people who were observing us.

When the stream of prospective foster parents dried up, it was time to eat again. The whole time we were there the menu never changed; it was always the same, consisting of warm cereal and white bread; but I always looked forward to it and loved it.

The next day, the auditorium was again opened for the public to come and view or take home a possible foster child. It was the same process as the day before, with the prospective foster parents, usually women, walking around the bunks to find the child of their choice. A tall, haggard-looking woman with white hair, grey eyes, and a loud brazen voice stopped by our bunks looking at Waltraut.

136

"How old is the cute little girl?" She asked. Edith answered.

"She is four years old, but will be five in December."

The woman examined Waltraut's face as if she were for sale. Finally she nodded.

"I'll take her," she said.

The lady gave Edith her name, which was Frau Kaiser, and her address. She assured us that she would be good to our sister and would try to arrange for us to see each other often. Frau Kaiser motioned to the Red Cross nurse and said that she was taking Waltraut home.

Now there were only two of us left.

I gathered that the reason people only gave me stares and never asked if I wanted a home was that I looked too sickly and undernourished. The problem was that the people of Berlin had very little food for themselves and those who came for foster children probably thought they could not afford to give me the nutrition I needed to look like a healthy girl of age 9.

Food was in very short supply and everything was rationed using a system of ration cards. Unfortunately, some of those who came for a foster child did not do so out of a sense of kindness to orphan children, but because of the extra ration card that came with these children. For their own gain, in other words.

Not only did Berlin citizens suffer a severe housing shortage, but it also became the center point of all the deported people from the East. Before the war, the population of Berlin, Germany was 4.3 million. A few months after the war ended, in August 1945, the population of Berlin had shrunk to 2.8 million. With all the refugees entering Berlin after the war ended and the returnees from the Eastern boundaries, the population began to gradually increase, even though housing was simply unavailable.

After the surrender in May 1945 half of all houses were damaged and one-third were uninhabitable – as much as 6 square miles of the city was simply rubble. There were at least one million people in Berlin who were completely homeless, living in the ruins. It took many years to solve the housing shortage, and for a long time every family who lived in a home with more than one room had to share their living space with other families. Sometimes three families had to live in a three room apartment or home, sharing the same kitchen.

This once beautiful capital city was now nothing but ruins and rubble. Some people had made homes for themselves in the ruins. If they could find four walls somewhere in the ruins, they would board up the windows and make it their home, since glass was also largely unobtainable. Power had to be severely rationed, and most people could count on electricity and water for only two hours in the morning and two hours at night. Everyone had to hurry and use these resources wisely when they were available.

Edith and I had remained unadopted in our temporary home in the gymnasium for two weeks when a distinctive-looking lady approached me one day and asked if I would like to make a home for myself with her family, which consisted of a mother, father, and a big brother named Manfred.

The lady was very distinguished looking. Her grey hair was neatly waved. She had grey eyes, a friendly smile, and she was well-dressed. I nodded my head "yes" and told her briefly that I had two younger sisters who had already been placed with families and that I wished to stay in touch with them as soon as I learned to find my way to them.

She assured me that she had no objections and that she would help me find where they lived. I kissed Edith good-bye and told her that we must try to see each other whenever we could. Edith had tears in her eyes.

"Sure Rita," she said, "don't worry, we're all in the same city and if I have to walk all night, I will come to find you, that I know."

Edith and I had become very close since the disappearance of our parents. Together we had sustained our little family to keep ourselves from starving. We both felt the pain when we last saw our father as a prisoner of the Russians, and now we had to say good-bye to each other.

Sadness was creeping upon me. My throat felt tight and I fought back the tears. I did not want the strange lady to see me cry for she might not want me then. I wanted to give her the impression that I was grateful to have a home with her. I did not look back, for if I had seen Edith's sad face with tears rolling down her cheeks, I would have not been able to hold back my own tears and would have sobbed uncontrollably, which might have ruined my chance to go home with this lady, who was Frau Hegemann.

She held me by the hand and walked me over to the desk, where my name was recorded as living with the Hegemann family in Berlin. And so we left.

Chapter 24

Arriving at my new home, I was very impressed with the beautiful space that they occupied. Their apartment was quite large, and had two bedrooms, a living room, a kitchen, and its own bathroom. No other family shared their space – I later found that this was highly unusual, and was most likely because they were members of the Communist Party and part of the governing class.

The kitchen was large and spotless. The adjoining living room was spacious with expensive furniture, on the floor laid and oriental rug. The master bedroom was furnished with a large, highly polished bedstead and other bulky pieces of furniture which completed the suite. Against the wall stood a small bed, which Frau Hegemann explained was made up for me. She then told me to come and meet my big brother.

As we walked along the corridor of the apartment, she opened the door which led into a small room. Up from the bed jumped Manfred, my new big brother. With his hand stretched out, he welcomed me to the family and proceeded to show me his hobbies, which were a fish aquarium he took pride in and some electric devices he had built like a telephone which he could use to communicate with his friend who lived in the same building on another floor.

After his initial friendliness, however, he mainly kept to himself in his room, busily working with his hobbies. Since I had not been blessed with the good fortune of having a brother, and was accustomed only to sisters, I felt very shy and awkward around him. He was 15 years old and thereby out of my age range; he could not be my playmate and I knew that he felt the same toward me.

After I had been introduced to Manfred and shown the house, Frau Hegemann wasted no time and showed me to the bathroom. She drew a warm bath for me, and gave me strict orders not to get out of the water until she had taken care of my infested hair and clothes. As I stripped myself of the clothes I had worn for almost a year, she picked up every piece carefully and burned them in the kitchen stove. She then cut my hair, washed what was left, and rubbed my scalp with kerosene. The kerosene burned my scalp like fire for I too had developed head sores from the lice.

After I had bathed, I was handed a pair of pajamas that had belonged to Manfred at one time. They fit just about right and, with a turban on my head, I was now put to bed. Laying in that strange bed, not having my sisters with me, I felt lonely and depressed. Somehow it did not feel quite like home, in my heart.

I tried to decide why I was not happy. Everything seemed so very good. Frau Hegemann had done all these things to help me; they weren't in need of my ration card and must have taken me in out of a desire to help. She had washed my body and cleaned my hair. The house was as fine as the chimney sweep master's, but still I felt empty inside.

The next morning, I laid in my bed looking around the room. It looked so elegant and clean. I could smell the kerosene from my hair; I was happy that I had no lice in my hair, as well as on my body. But I still had the same empty feeling that I dared not show to these people. I was afraid to move about the house with the turban on my head, as I thought that the boy might laugh at my appearance – and besides, how could I ever think of them as my family?

Frau Hegemann must have heard that I had awakened, for she walked into the room and greeted me cheerily.

"Good morning! Did you sleep well?" She asked.

I just nodded my head yes, for no words could come out of my mouth. She then asked me to come into the kitchen to meet my new father. My face became flushed and I felt delirious with fright. As slowly as possible, with the turban on my head smelling strongly of kerosene, I walked into the kitchen. There on the chair sat a tall, dark-haired man with a slim build. He stretched his long bony hand out to me and with a forced grin he said, "Welcome to our family, Rita." Then there was silence, for I did not answer.

He struck up a conversation with me and said that he was a dentist and his place of work was across the street, to which I had little to say. Frau Hegemann now interceded and held up a dress she had sat up all night to sew for me. Also, she had managed to fabricate underwear. She then opened a cabinet and pulled out a box which contained one shoe. She asked me to try on the shoe, and we found that it fit perfectly. She went on to say that during the bombing of Berlin, on one of her trips to the bomb shelter, she had found the one shoe laying on the street, and thought to keep it. Since it fit so well, she would have another made for me out of a brown leather bag they had. I shyly thanked her and again I was lost for anything else to say.

Herr Hegemann pulled me over to him by the arm and asked if I would like to live with his family. I nodded my head yes. He then asked me to address him as "father" and his wife as "mother." At his request call them mother and father, I felt more lost than ever.

142

I thought to myself, how can I possibly call strangers by "mother" and "father"? They are not my parents. I have parents, and even if my parents were dead, I could not substitute these people for my own parents! No, I thought, they cannot ask that of me.

Frau Hegemann then unwrapped the turban and checked my head. She said that just to be sure, they would make the same application once more that night. So again that night, I slept with the unpleasant aroma of kerosene.

In days to come, it became necessary for me to resume my schooling. Frau Hegemann had asked the principal of the local school to enroll me in the fourth grade, which was where my age cohort belonged, but I had actually only completed second grade because of the war. I had lost one year in East Prussia, and so the fourth grade was a puzzle to me.

There were 56 other children enrolled in my class. Our teacher, Frau Braun, was pleasant, not strict, and I could get lost among all the children and just daydream. I spent my time in class looking out the window into the distant horizon, thinking about the time I had lived in my hometown of Osterode.

In my thoughts, I could ride on my beautiful roller scooter. I could see my father as we walked hand in hand from the Easter Egg Hunt. I could see my dear mother sitting on the oven bench knitting her red sweater. Now, if only in my dreams, I could have all the things I was longing for.

The faces of my parents were imprinted in my mind. They were photographs in my mind that never changed. They looked pleasantly on me, as if saying, "Wait for us."

After walking home from school, there were chores waiting for me. Every day the chores were the same. After walking into the spotless kitchen, I dried the dishes which were waiting for me in a tray. For two hours I was expected to play outside. My play outside consisted of wandering the streets, looking at empty stores, and daydreaming constantly. I thought in my wanderings, that luck might bring me face to face with one of my dear sisters.

I felt unhappy with the life I now lived. I could not get close to the people that had given me a home. I was not able to live the ordered existence that was expected of me, not after Edith and I had lived free and wild, like animals, exploring ruins for food, hoarding milk, begging for bread, and being exposed to rape, shootings, killings, hunger, dirt, and flames for a year.

Frau Hegemann always had food on the table. Her husband would often get paid for his work with vegetables, bread or small amounts of meat that was then more valuable than money. So mealtimes were a pleasure. On the other hand, the most dreadful time for me was bedtime. During the day, I could avoid saying "mother" to Frau Hegemann, but at night, I was always reminded to address both with "good night, mother, and good night, father" each time. I became frustrated; the blood came rushing into my face, and I could hardly stumble the greeting out. I became more withdrawn.

Herr and Frau Hegemann both belonged to the Communist Party and so did not believe in God; instead, on Sunday morning, they attended a concert that consisted of classical string music and arias that were sung by middle aged men and women, with lyrics that I could not understand. I would sit with them through two hours of Brahms and Beethoven feeling bored to no end.

After a few of these concerts, I asked if I could be allowed to attend church instead. The Hegemanns responded with frowns, and told me that I could run to church every Sunday if I wanted, but tried to encourage me to learn to enjoy the music of the great composers because it was educational. They told me that the teachings of religion do not pertain to realistic thinking, and that it was all based on myth.

The next Sunday before they began getting ready for the concert, I put on my best Sunday dress and announced that I was going to church. Frau Hegemann gave a faint smile and said, "Just go." Alone, I walked to the church. The church was very tall, with a steeple 100 feet high. The outside was scarred by fire and bomb fragment impacts, but the inside had not been damaged by the bombs, and mosaic art covered the huge ceiling, including a beautiful picture of Jesus and his disciples.

The minister stood at the podium dressed in black, with a large cross hanging from his neck down to the middle of his robe. When the organ music stopped playing, the minister lifted his arms to preach and his wide sleeves fanned out in the traditional manner of our German gospel preachers.

It was mid-summer, and we approached the end of school year. One day a group of people came into the classroom, among them a doctor, a nurse, and the principal of the school. Standing in front of the class, one of them pointed his finger directly at me, and turning to the teacher, asked her to record my name; after me he chose four other children. They didn't say what this signified, but after the group left the classroom, Frau Braun announced that the Board of Health had chosen five lucky children to spend the summer on a farm, and that we would be notified by mail and told the whereabouts of our destination.

I felt elated. For the first time, I bubbled over with conversation, telling my foster parents about the happy event. They felt happy for me, and told me that the reason I was chosen is because of my undernourished appearance.

Frau Hegemann immediately started to plan to sew for me a wardrobe of dresses and pajamas. At that time during the long recovery from the war, one could not buy material in a store, and she had to take material from old dresses of hers to make new ones for me.

When at last the time had come for my departure, Frau Hegemann accompanied me to the train station, and with a few words of advice to write very soon, we said good-bye. I was to be gone for six weeks.

Chapter 25

Approximately 50 children occupied the passenger train, which was to take us to the rich farm county of Stralsund, approximately 100 kilometers north of Berlin. Hurriedly, I found and occupied a window seat in order to observe the beautiful countryside as it rolled by. On this beautiful warm summer day the train rolled out of the station leaving behind the ruins of Berlin.

Open to my view were the open meadows and fields changing color with their fruits and grains soon to be harvested. I was encouraged by this bounty, not realizing that much of this abundance was owed in debt by the German people to their conquerors.

Unlike the train of our deportation from Poland which barely moved two hours per day, we arrived nonstop at our destination in the early evening of the same day. At the Stralsund train station we were met by town officials, and were distributed in groups of 15 to various parts of the area. All the children belonging to the same group as I were guided by the mayor of the town to a horse-drawn carriage, and we were driven down a road, with one of us let off each time at a selected farm. At each farm, the mayor led each child to be introduced to the farmers who would watch over them.

After the last child had been delivered, the mayor turned to me, and with a sympathetic smile, he told me what he had in mind for me, which was the largest farm in that part of the country. He said that there I would be in good hands, for the couple had no children of their own, and would see to it that I departed from them healthy and strong. This reminded me that in the eyes of adults I appeared to be suffering from starvation, even though I didn't feel bad off at all.

As the horse cart drove into the large yard, two middle-aged people came quickly to welcome me. The mayor explained to them that I had been especially chosen to spend the summer on their farm, for I seemed to be the one most deprived of normal weight.

The lady, a pleasant brunette, lovingly put her arm on my shoulder, and with a smile, assured the mayor that she would surely try to fatten me up. With that, the mayor departed and the couple led me into their house.

Herr and Frau Reinhard asked about my background, and this led to the tale of our family tragedy in East Prussia and the separation of my parents along with my sisters thereafter. The couople listened with great sympathy. When I was done explaining my history, Frau Reinhard took my hand in hers and told me she wished so that I could stay on with them as their daughter. I felt sincere warmth radiating from her, and knew immediately that I would have loved to stay.

I spent six glorious weeks in the idyllic wonder of nature. I was free to roam the fields as I pleased. I visited the other big farms nearby and watched swallows build their nests out of hard clay, and on top of the nearby farmhouse, on a wagon wheel set up on the roof horizontally for the purpose, a pair of storks were tending their young which laid in a big nest made out of straw. I was allowed and even encouraged to visit their kitchen garden at any time to pick fruit and vegetables of all kinds to eat.

I did not see all that much of Herr and Frau Reinhard, for their day began at 4 a.m. and they spent the whole day working in the fields. My day began much later, and when I awoke in the morning the table in my room was always set with the most delicious breakfast imaginable: boiled eggs, salami, bread, butter and milk. There was so much that I could never eat such anywhere near all of it. I thought of my sisters, and how I would have loved to share all this with them. I considered saving some of the food in my suitcase to take to them, but I knew it would not keep. It did not seem real to me that I could suddenly eat eggs, salami, and drink real milk! This food was not obtainable in Berlin. Dinner was if anything even better, with good quantities of meat, potatoes and vegetables; of the meat there was various forms of pork, including bacon and ham, and fowl. There were even pastries!

I thought of how lucky these people were, and wondered if they realized that they had everything. I remember the days on the farm as always being sunny. The world seemed enveloped in a big package of sunshine and carefree happiness, without ruins, without discontentment and pain, and most of all without loneliness.

I felt happy and serene sitting on a fence post to just stare into the distance. I could watch the trees sway in the wind and listen to the songbirds chirping. My mind could wander into the world of illusion and go home to be with my natural family. I could clearly see the kind face of my grandmother and I could be with her. For a moment, I could substitute reality for my daydreams. When my mind jerked back to reality, I always felt disappointed. It had all felt so very real, and I wished that I could stay in that world of dreams a little while longer.

In the evenings, I accompanied Frau Reinhard to tend her livestock. She gave fresh hay to the cows and watered

149

their stalls. Together we gathered eggs from the chickens and threw them some grain. We had conversations about the animals and she would tell me of her favorite, which was a cow; she was the favorite because she gave more milk than all the others.

She often told me that she wished I could stay, but this could not be. I had to go back as scheduled, and nothing could change this outside of a complicated legal process which was unlikely to succeed. If it were indeed impossible for me to stay, nevertheless I felt pleased that she cared to have me.

On one occasion, Herr Reinhardt asked if I would like to ride with his horse cart into town. So early that morning, we departed to arrive in the town of Stralsund at noon. There, as a treat, he showed me into a guesthouse and ordered for me a malt beer, which reminded me of my arrival in Berlin, and the beginning of an era which separated me from my sisters.

Time will not stand still, and too quickly my summer vacation came to an end. Frau Reinhardt lovingly made a package of good salami and bread for me to take home. When it came time for me to leave, she put me on the scale to see how much I now weighed, and happily announced that from my arrival weight of 41 pounds, I now weighed 47! She assured me that it made a great difference in my appearance, and that now I had a rosy face instead of the ghostly white I had when I arrived. As she hugged me good-bye, she encouraged me to have hope that I would soon be reunited with my parents and my sisters. She then gave me their address and said to stay in touch.

Herr Reinhardt helped with my packages and we took a seat in his horse cart that drove us to the train station.

Thinking back, it seemed like it had been lifetime that I had been privileged to spend on their farm. I did not at all feel inhibited at their presence but had come to love these people. I vowed to myself that I *would* stay in touch with them.

The conductor now blew his whistle, and the train began to move; my happy and carefree days had ended.

Chapter 26

Arriving back in Berlin, I felt a little spark of happiness, for here was the home of my sisters. Someday, I thought, we will visit with each other and I will have lots to tell them about my summer on the farm.

It was Herr Hegemann who came to meet me. When he saw me, he was seemed pleasantly surprised at my appearance, and told me how good it had been for me to spend the summer on the farm, and that my face had taken on a healthy color.

Arriving home, I found that Frau Hegemann was confined to her bed; she had taken ill and was suffering from a blood clot in her leg. She welcomed me home with a grim face, from the pain that she told me she was suffering. I felt sorry for her, but that old feeling of inhibition in her presence started to creep up on me. I couldn't offer even the simplest words of sympathy, like "I am sorry that you are ill, mother," because of the pressure I immediately felt to call her "mother." Instead, I just stood staring at her, fishing for proper words of sympathy, ones that omitted "mother," but in vain

As I stood before her, she finally broke the silence and told me that she had a nice surprise. The surprise was that this weekend I was to visit with both Edith and Irmgard.

At the announcement, the ice started to melt in me and I rushed over to her bed asking how she had managed to arrange the visit. She told me that the Red Cross had sent her the address of their whereabouts and she in turn had contacted my sisters' foster parents to arrange the visit.

So here it was that on Sunday, I dressed in my best clothes and set off to visit Irmgard at Unklischstrasse 57; it must have been a two-mile walk. After I asked people for directions, I arrived at the large apartment house where Irmgard now lived. I walked up to the fourth floor and found the door with a bright, polished copper door knob. I read the name, which was George Bach, turned the doorbell, and waited for a response. Shortly there were footsteps coming toward me, the door opened, and with a warm smile, Frau Bach invited me in.

Now, I heard little footsteps running out from another room. Irmgard stood before me, and there smiling in the background was Edith. She walked toward me and as we all embraced she said, "I am so happy to see you Rita, how are you?" I immediately told them that I had been chosen to spend a wonderful summer at a distant farm and to top it off I was overjoyed to be able to spend the day with my sisters.

Edith explained that she was now able to visit Irmgard whenever time allowed, because Frau Bach had persuaded a neighbor to give her a home to be a playmate for her only daughter. Although Edith revealed that the woman plainly showed partiality toward her daughter by secretly rewarding her with treats and kind words, but had neither for Edith.

Frau Bach had planned to make our reunion a special occasion by sharing with us her dinner, which had to be provided from her meager ration card, and to top it off, she managed to bake a cake. We spent a wonderful day together. Frau Bach told us how she had come to love Irmgard like her own flesh and blood and that she had sewn

Irmgard a wardrobe by tearing apart her bed sheets so that she could have decent clothes to start school in. She plainly doted on Irmgard, and it showed: Irmgard was always smiling, and her big blue eyes clearly said that she had found a happy home. Every now and then she threw her little arms around the neck of Frau Bach, not just because she felt grateful but because she had found a loving mother in her.

Far from the time when we had had to cut off all of Irmgard's hair to rid it of lice, now she had grown a beautiful head of dark shiny hair that she wore in page-boy style. Frau Bach commented that when her hair reached the proper length, Irmgard would wear it in curly locks like Shirley Temple. I felt happy for her, although I was also a little envious, wishing that I too could have such a feeling of belonging and warmth toward my foster parents.

For weeks, Frau Hegemann was in bed with phlebitis. Frequently during the day a nurse would come to look after her needs. On one occasion, I happened to overhear Frau Hegemann voicing her opinion about me to the nurse. She told her that she could no longer keep me on in her household. She said she had hoped that I would adjust to her family better than I had, and that she did not care for my restrained character. She was even now making arrangements to have me placed elsewhere.

At hearing this, my heart started pounding and blood rushed into my head as I realized that I would soon be leaving this family. It was no longer my home, I thought, but then, it never had been.

What would they do with me? Where would I go? That night I could not sleep. Like a motion picture, I relived my 10 years of life. I started to pray, remembering the humble words of my grandmother as she instructed me not to show greed in prayer, but to ask only for absolute needs. I told the Lord that I loved my dear parents with all my heart and very desperately needed them.

"Oh, Dear God," I prayed, "I will not try to be greedy and ask for them both. That would mean the indescribable happiness that we could only experience in your heaven, so please grant me my plea and send home the one I need most, my mother."

In order to pray personally to God I conceived the image in my mind of kneeling in front of His throne, beneath his feet, with my head bowed. I prayed to him over and over. Even with my head bowed, I could see in the face of God that He understood. In my mind, I could see my father stepping back so that I could choose my mother over him, and I could feel that he approved. As I became tired from prayer, my last thoughts were directed to my father. I asked him to forgive me, for I felt that the Lord would turn away from me if I greedily asked for everything. In spirit, I told him that I loved him, that he was my home and my protector, and that I would never forget him until the end of time.

From that day on, I made prayer my daily practice. I felt very strongly that the Lord was listening. He told me to be patient. To this day the image of the Lord has stayed fixed in my mind the same way as it was when I was 10 years old.

Within the week of hearing that I was to leave the Hegemann household, I found myself placed in one of the orphan homes operated by the city of Berlin. Arriving at the home, I was led by a young nurse to the offices. There they filled out the intake forms with my personal information, issued me a set of clean clothes, and then a woman dressed in white took me to the quarters that I was to share with fifteen other girls from school age up to fifteen years old. She assigned a bunk to me, and then without a word of encouragement from her, she left and there I stayed.

If found that the girls in my ward were friendly and pleasant towards me. Some of them asked why I had been placed there and what had happened to my family, and so I briefly told them the story of my life to that point. It turned out that they all had similar stories.

Living in the orphan home, all the girls including me felt detached from the world. We were not allowed to step outside the walls of the home until we were released to go to a foster home. It seemed like being locked up in a jail. The windows were equipped with bars, and the doors leading into each ward were also kept locked. This multi-story building wrapped around a courtyard that was cut off from the outside world by a huge brick wall with only one exit and an iron gate. When I asked the girls in my ward why we were so isolated and why the doors were kept locked, they told me with a laugh, as if I were ignorant, "So you won't run away, Rita!"

The morning after my arrival a nurse came into the ward, called out my name and asked me to come with her. She ushered me into a medical examination room in which the doctor was seated and waiting for me. As he gave me a routine checkup, the nurse recorded with a pencil all the specifics on her pad. Standing before the doctor, stripped of all my clothes, he had me lie on the table with my knees raised and my legs apart. He then took a specimen to check for venereal disease.

Being just 10 years old, I found it to be the most embarrassing situation I had ever encountered. At the time, it was not explained to me what the doctor was doing or what he was looking for, but as I got older, I found that the checkup was considered necessary because the Russian troops had the bad reputation in Germany of raping females of all ages, from child to grandmother, and that venereal diseases had taken an epidemic toll.

The food in the orphanage was good, but it was the only pleasurable thing to look forward to. The building was

156

large, but I had no idea of how many children were housed therein, for I had no contact with anyone except the children in my ward.

Electricity in Berlin was still conserved and in short supply, so the rule was that at the onset of evening we must be settled in bed. This was because electricity for light was only available for a few hours in the evening.

Some of the girls occupied themselves with singing sad melodies. Their lyrics spoke of home, parents, and love. Listening to the lyrics brought sadness to many of us. Often I could hear children crying into their pillows. The isolation from the outside world was hard on us all. The only sound of civilization we could hear was the street car passing by which gave a ding before it set in motion. Again, it could only be heard but not seen.

In all the months I lived in that children's home, I never received a visitor or even mail, until one day. A social worker entered my ward and told me to get dressed and gather up all my personal belongings. Contemplating the thought that I might be transferred to a better establishment with more freedom, I felt happy.

I was escorted out into an office where I recognized Frau Kaiser, the foster mother of my youngest sister, Waltraut. With a stretched out hand, she greeted me and said that she had decided to take me to her home to be with Waltraut. I told her how happy it made me to be able to live with my sister and that I was grateful for her decision.

After a long time of being deprived of my freedom, I could finally join the whirl of the city. It felt so good to walk along the sidewalks and see the trees, to watch people walking by, and to ride on the street car. I could not wait to see the face of my dear little sister.

Chapter 27

Arriving at the four-story apartment house, I found that Frau Kaiser lived on the third floor. As we walked into the kitchen of her apartment, I saw that there was a small round table, and on a chair sitting next to the table was little Waltraut. With a faint smile, she said, "Hi, Rita." Her eyes were deep blue and sad. Her face looked pale, and she did not look very happy.

Frau Kaiser, with a boisterous but kidding voice, ordered me to make myself at home. She assured me that Waltraut and I would be much happier from now on; that was the reason for having me, so that we sisters could be together. Also, with an extra ration card, it would make it easier to manage the food budget.

Frau Kaiser's was a simple-looking two room apartment. The living room was divided into a living room at one end and a bedroom at the other. Waltraut and I shared a twin bed which stood pushed alongside the wall. The kitchen was equipped with a coal stove and a gas burner, a china hutch, and that small children's table as well as a regular-sized table.

Frau Kaiser had vices like smoking cigarettes, and she loved good coffee made from real coffee beans. These luxuries were very difficult to obtain in Berlin, especially in the Soviet sector where we were, and so a lively black market dealing with such goods had sprung up.

So it happened that one day, not long after I took up residence in her house, Frau Kaiser clipped off some food coupons from our ration cards, handed them to me in an envelope and told me to go to an address she scribbled on a piece of paper. There I was to exchange the contents of the envelope for a pack of cigarettes, and I was to hurry.

Obeying her orders, I did as she asked and brought her the cigarettes. Other times, with food coupons as an exchange, I received coffee beans. Frau Kaiser made it a special event. After Waltraut and I went to sleep, she loved to enjoy the fine ground coffee she brewed and with it she would smoke the precious cigarettes. Because of this diversion of our food rations, food for Waltraut and myself became very meager. Often, we had to survive on one piece of bread a day. The cigarettes and coffee for Frau Kaiser had to be there for her to enjoy each day.

It was summertime, so I was often in mind of searching for food as I had done in Prussisch Holland. But in Berlin, it was a different matter. All houses, sometimes even those in ruins, were occupied by people just as hungry as I was. I tried searching for gardens which had fruit trees, but this wasn't very fruitful. Often, as I searched I was driven away by the owners of the property and even so most of the fruit that hung low had already been picked.

Walking the streets of Berlin, everything was barren. Stores opened only when the food available for ration cards arrived. Then it became my job to stand in endless lines and wait for hours to be waited on. Often standing in a long line just reaching the entrance of the store, the manager would announce that he had run out of supplies and to come back when the sign in the window said that more food was available. On those occasions, some people became angry, some cried, but it didn't matter – nobody could do anything but walk away. I learned from experience that I must get past the entrance as quickly as I could so that I could be waited on before it was too late. As small as I was, I could sometimes sneak and wiggle to the front of the line. Often this worked for me, but sometimes I was found and pushed to the end of the line by the other people.

The food that was received with the ration card had to last for one decade, which meant a ten-day supply. Needless to say, it never lasted more than two to three days and then there was nothing. I also noticed that my foster parents ate the better food at night so we could not see them. It angered me but I was afraid of accusing them for fear they would separate me from my sister.

Many times in the summer, I collected cherry pits which I found on the sidewalk or by the curb. After collecting a handful, I would find a stone and crack open the cherry stone and eat the seed inside. Even better was to find cores of apples that people had discarded; brushing off the dirt, I would eat them with the seeds and only dispose of the stems.

Frau Kaiser continued to exchange our food stamps for cigarettes and coffee. It seemed to be so unfair, for my little sister, only years old had shriveled to skin and bones, and so did I once more.

Winter arrived in Berlin. It was the coldest winter I had ever known, and many people in Berlin were found starved and frozen to death in their beds. All the wood to be had was stolen by people and burned to keep warm. Park benches, wooden fences, even the wooden casings that enclosed the electric wires of the commuter train was gone, leaving them exposed. People stood hovered around the flames of gas stoves rubbing their hands together to keep warm. The gas flames were virtually useless for they only warmed the hands and not the body.

One day, I saw a boy carrying several briquettes of coal. When I asked him where he had obtained such a treasure, he confided in me that he and many other people stole them at the train station right off the freight cars. He said that anyone could do it, but if were to try he cautioned me that I had to be alert so as not to get caught by the police.

The next day, I set out with a canvas bag to steal briquettes. Off to the side of the train station, hidden between the ruins, were many people, including the boy who had told me about the place. He instructed me what I must be aware of and when to run from the police.

The train carrying the coal started to come in but stopped outside the station, directly across from our hideout. The people now set in motion and raced as fast as they could across the tracks, carefully jumping over the bare wires of the commuter train. Two or three young men hurriedly climbed upon the train and threw briquettes to the ground as the others collected as many as they could stuff into their burlap sacks.

I gathered twenty of them but then found that I could not lift my sack. Suddenly, I noticed that everyone was starting to scatter, jumping over the wires to get back to the other side when I heard the police whistles blowing. In vain, I tried not to leave my so desperately needed briquettes behind when I heard a voice behind me telling me to run.

There was my young friend, and with one hand holding his sack and his other picking up one end of mine, together we made it to the other side. He then helped me to carry them home, but told me not to take that many the next time because it could get me in serious trouble. He also cautioned me that I must not touch the wires for I could get electrocuted. These were the bare wires carrying electricity for the commuter trains – wires which used to be covered by wooden casing but the casing stolen to burn.

Frau Kaiser was elated to see me bring home enough

briquettes to stay warm all day. I assured her that I would bring home almost that much every day so we could keep warm. Each briquette weighed one pound and the most I could carry by myself was barely ten pounds.

It felt like heaven to be able to sit in the small kitchen with the iron cover of the stove turning red hot. I vowed to myself that I would go twice a day to have enough. From that day forward, my days started at the train station, waiting for the coal train to arrive. Waltraut would also join me sometimes, but she couldn't carry much, so she was stationed as a lookout whose job it was to watch out for the approach of the police. When she saw them coming, she was supposed to shout out "Dicke Luft!" This means "thick air" in English, and was Berlin slang for "the police are coming!"

Frau Kaiser was lucky and found a job at a slaughter house in the stockyards of East Berlin. With her being gone to work each day, Waltraut and I were left locked in the apartment alone. Frau Kaiser would give us our daily ration of bread, usually one slice; sometimes it was spread with lard and other times it was without. The bread had to last us until Frau Kaiser arrived home. Of course, one of the "benefits" of her new job was that she had an opportunity to pilfer from the slaughter house. Although stealing at the stockyard was forbidden and anyone caught was fired and even imprisoned, supervision there was loose enough that she was never caught. On her return each day, she frequently emptied her bra of chicken feet, calves feet, brains, and even pieces of beef.

Most times she exchanged the beef for coffee or cigarettes on the black market, but the pig's feet she strippod of thoir hoofo and mado dclicious ooup, seasoned with salt and thickened with flour. The chicken feet were cooked in the same fashion but she made a sweet and sour dish from the brains. The food now varied somewhat and

162

everything tasted good. Still, late at night Herr and Frau Kaiser ate the better cuts of meat that she could steal without sharing with us.

Chapter 28

One day, Frau Kaiser gave Waltraut and I the wonderful news that she would take our sister Edith into her house. Edith had become disenchanted with her placement in her previous foster mother and demanded to leave her house. Edith had become the ward of the juvenile authorities and had been placed in an orphanage.

When the lady from the juvenile authority investigated Frau Kaiser's home, she determined that it was unsuitable, for there were the four of us living in already very small quarters. Frau Kaiser pleaded with the woman to change her determination because she said she was so very concerned for us three girls and her only intention was to have the three sisters together all in one dwelling. Frau Kaiser then carefully suggested that if the placement could be approved, it would mean a loaf of bread to her as a token of our appreciation. Before the investigator left the apartment, Frau Kaiser handed her our bread and shook her hand good-bye.

A week later, the happy event occurred – Edith arrived. She had grown since I had seen her, and had now reached the age of 12. Her hair was blond and straight, her face had a rosy color, and when she smiled her teeth appeared to have grown in evenly and white. Truly, the three of us were now reunited and I felt grateful to Frau Kaiser for that.

Edith and I spent many hours reminiscing about our various foster homes and the people with whom we had shared quarters. Edith, being critical and mistrusting, complained to me that the people who took children into their homes did it for no other reason other than to benefit by it. If they could prove to the government a large head count in one household, it would mean that they no longer had to share a home with another smaller family. The housing shortage was so critical that every home owner with more than one room and a kitchen would have to give up additional rooms to one or more families.

As far as the food was concerned, the extra ration card that came with the extra child brought additional food into the house, but that the foster child didn't always receive it! Edith bitterly informed me that in her previous foster home the lady secretly fed the better food to her own daughter but not any to her. In contrast, she knew that Herr and Frau Bach took Irmgard into their home out of goodness and not profit. I had to agree with her, and also had to confide to her that the same situation existed in our present environment – that Frau Kaiser saved the better food for herself, and to top it off, she traded our needed ration cards for unnecessary luxuries such as coffee and cigarettes.

The next morning, Edith and I set out for the train station to wait for the daily freight train loaded with briquettes. By now I knew all the angles and explained the hazards to her, just as I had been taught by my friend. We had managed to collect a number of briquettes, when, as usual, we heard police whistles blowing. And here were two policemen running towards the crowd of people with their billy clubs waving in the air. We picked up our bag, and began running in the opposite direction from the police.

Suddenly, the commuter train started to leave the station, and it was going to block us from escape! In vain, Edith and I tried to beat the train, jumping across the hot wires. Edith screamed to me to drop the briquettes, as the load was causing us to move too slowly. She grabbed onto my hand and together we made it to the other side.

Standing there, gasping for breath, Edith in detail pointed out the danger of what we had just tried to do. We could get electrocuted by the wires when being chased by the police, we could be killed by the commuter train which passed the tracks every ten minutes, or we could get caught by the police and go to jail! She expressed great displeasure for my foolishness in endangering my life for the sake of pleasing my foster parents, who didn't really care for us except as meal tickets. She further went on saying that no one should take advantage of either our health or strength or the innocence of our youth.

She declared that she had no intention of cooperating with any adult assuming authority to impose unfairness upon any of us. "Look at you," she scolded, "there is nothing left of you but skin and bones. I can see you have no will power to say no. You let people take advantage of you for the sake of having a place to live. It will be different from now on. I will not allow them to eat our food at night or exchange our bread for coffee or cigarettes. I will confront Frau Kaiser and take the risk of being tossed back into the orphanage."

I replied to Edith that yes it was a bad situation but it wasn't so bad as all that. I insisted that it was worth it to go along, as long as we could be together. As to the food, perhaps we could also find gardens and fields to get fruit or vegetables as soon as summer arrived, just as we had done in East Prussia.

Edith dismissed this thought by saying that she would love to live like we did in East Prussia and that she was perfectly capable of managing our family. All we

166

needed was one room, our own ration cards, and some money from the government to buy food. But the bureaucrats wouldn't allow such an arrangement; instead they severed our only ties and handed us over to the greedy vultures called foster parents.

Responding to my begging her not to rock the boat about the ration cards and so forth, Edit reluctantly agreed to leave the matter alone for the time being.

Upon arrival at our apartment, we found pleasant visitors: Frau Bach and Irmgard had stopped by to visit. Irmgard looked clean and healthy. She smiled a happy smile as she saw us enter the house. Her dark hair had grown long and was now curled into pretty corkscrew curls. She wore a pretty white pleated shirt and a blouse which Frau Bach had sewn for her out of a bedsheet. She truly looked like a beautiful mannequin out of a magazine.

Edith took advantage of the opportunity to complain to Frau Bach about the ruthlessness of Frau Kaiser. Frau Bach listened sympathetically without endorsing or disapproving what Edith was saying.

As she was seated in the kitchen chair, I noticed that her face looked grayish pale and her eyes appeared sunken into her sockets. She spoke as though it were a great effort, and now and then she closed her eyes for a moment. When I asked if she did not feel well, she replied that outside of having a slight headache, she felt fine. She had come to invite the three of us to spend Sunday with Irmgard. Also, she was planning to have us for dinner at her house.

I always loved to visit Irmgard, for Frau Bach radiated warmth that only a mother could have for her child. She always tried to have some kind of nice food for us. She knew how to make potato peelings into a tasty dish. She could make spinach from dandelions and fried vegetable roots to make them taste like meat.

On some of those occasions we were allowed to stay as long as we liked. Often, together with Herr & Frau Bach,

167

we sat in her clean living room and reminisced about our parents and our homeland. Frau Bach never failed to encourage us not to abandon the hope that one day our parents would return and we would be reunited.

Having extended the invitation to visit, Frau Bach now turned to leave with Irmgard. As she forced a warm smile to say good-bye she sank to her knees and collapsed in the doorway. Edith and I helped her onto the bed. Sitting looking faint on the bed with her eyes open, she confessed to us that lately she had very little food to eat and it was just weakness that had befallen her.

Suddenly, I recalled many times Frau Bach saying that the young come before the old, for they need energy to grow. I remember when food was served at her table she would not sit with us. She gave her portions to Irmgard and she herself ate very little or nothing at all. She sacrificed her meager rations to share with all of us and as a result she herself had gone hungry. I could plainly see that Irmgard did not suffer, for she looked healthy with rosy cheeks and her eyes sparkling with happiness and contentment. Like a saint disregarding her own needs, Frau Bach unselfishly catered to her foster child.

Chapter 29

The springtime of 1947 had arrived, and Berlin still lay in ruins. Food was as scarce as ever and people continued to suffer from typhoid fever and cholera which was brought on by dirt, contaminated water, and insects; although we were free of lice before coming to the Kaisers, both lice and bed bugs seemed to gather in masses in this apartment, and became a new problem.

During the day the pests were rarely visible, but at night they tormented me to no end. My body developed red welts and scratches all over my skin. The disease was called "Russian Impetigo" in Berlin, and the blisters spread all over my arms, legs, and body. Some healed, but others became infected before they healed, leaving an ugly scaling crust, as large as pennies all over my arms and legs.

After a year, the disease itself disappeared, but the ugly blue blotches were visible for many years. Whenever I went swimming they became especially noticeable, for they turned a deep bluish purple, like polka dots, and attracted attention – people would stare at me and some even asked the nature of my purple blotches. Edith was also infected and the two of us became a spectacle at Erkner Beach in Berlin. The disease was treated with sulfa salve, but it was a long process. Some of the crusty scales dried up and new blisters appeared in other places. By the time I had grown into adulthood, the blue rings on my body had turned pale brown and faded into white specks that I still can identify.

Summertime is a blessing to all mankind. It can heal the body and lift the spirit. It warms the waters and gives us the opportunity to cleanse our bodies as often as we like. It never ceases to produce vegetables and grain. The earth had not suffered from the war but continued to bear food for all living things.

So as the summer arrived again, there were many gardens which we hoped would have an apple or pear tree with branches full of fruit low enough for us to reach. There were also gooseberry bushes, with their prickly branches squeezing through white picket fences. Their fruit turned light brown when ripe, and were juicy and sweet.

But the return of summer did not solve all human problems. Water and electricity was still rationed. It was always frustrating to be washing your hair and then suddenly have the water supply turn off. When this happened to me, the rest of the day I would have to walk around with sticky hair and it was most uncomfortable. The effects of Germany's requirement to pay some war reparations to the Soviet Union in the form of coal made it necessary to ration coal as well. This had effects at many levels, as for example at the beauty parlor, where besides paying for the service in money, each person had to bring one coal briquette – this helped to heat the water for shampooing. The uncertain electrical supply was also very annoying, since when sitting under the dryer, often the electricity would shut off and customers would be forced to walk home in curlers and come back the next day for a comb out.

Another activity that went on in spite of the season was the ongoing project of clearing the city of rubble, which all able-bodied adults were expected to participate in. This went on in towns and cities all throughout Germany, but this was especially evident in Berlin, having been terribly destroyed by bombing and artillery.

Walking through the streets of Berlin, I saw people wielding wheelbarrows, picks, shovels, and hammers. Because building materials were in short supply, each brick was cleaned of mortar, rinsed and stacked in a neat pile to be picked up by trucks and taken to build new buildings.

Some people were assigned to work on the rebuilding program for pay, but many others were working as volunteers through their employers, donating up to 500 hours to help in the rebuilding program on weekends and after working hours. The program started in early 1946 when I was only 10 years old and lasted until 1951. When I became a teenager I served as an apprentice in this program in the Communist section of Berlin. I was asked not *if* I would like to donate my free time to the rebuilding program, but *how many hours* I would donate. I dared not pledge one measly hour, so I told them that I would be glad to pledge 200 hours. This was something that I had to faithfully carry out, and my work was recorded by stamping a card each time I donated labor hours at this task.

Another problem in the city, because of the still-disrupted city systems, was disease, with cholera and typhoid fever very prominent. Many people also died every day of whooping cough and diphtheria – but tuberculosis became the number one killer. In response, East Germany launched an immunization program and it became mandatory for every citizen to be immunized. And for the Health Department to be certain that every citizen being immunized, it became law that proof of immunization was required before a citizen could receive ration cards.

Edith, Waltraut, and I had spent six months together living with Herr and Frau Kaiser. Although it was very comforting to have the three of us together under one roof, the Kaisers continued to use our ration cards to provide for their luxuries while feeding us very meagerly, and they continued to selfishly eat the better food in the evening when they thought were sound asleep. Because of my urging, Edith bore this unfair treatment very grudgingly for a time, but finally could not bear it any longer.

Once more Frau Kaiser handed Edith an envelope containing ration stamps that she wanted her to exchange for coffee and cigarettes. Edith's face turned red with anger, and with resentment in her voice she confronted Frau Kaiser. Edith told her that her conduct toward us was unfair and that we were aware of their nightly dining. She accused her of viciously undermining our health and our strength by taking advantage of our youth and the power that the State had given her over us. It was inexcusable, she told her, to take orphans into her tiny home with the intention of profiting from the extra ration cards that came with us, selfishly using the food that we were entitled to have, just to seek her own pleasure by selling it on the black market to obtain luxuries she could live without. She went on to declare that we would no longer risk our lives and possible jail time stealing coal from the train station. If she wanted the pleasure of keeping warm in the winter, she would have to find another way of obtaining heating materials.

Frau Kaiser was outraged by these accusations. She grabbed Edith by the back of her neck and struck her several times in her face. As Edith struggled to get free, Frau Kaiser grabbed a shoe and followed her into the other room striking her several times on the back, all the while yelling that she was most disrespectful toward her and certainly ungrateful for the good Frau Kaiser tried to do by reuniting the three of us in her home. With a red blotchy face, Edith now sobbed uncontrollably, and threatened that she would not let it rest but would go the juvenile authorities and

172

swear out a complaint against her. She shouted that she would rather go to an orphanage, where at least everyone was treated on an equal basis, than stay under this roof.

I was emotionally shaken and I knew something had to change after today. I was sure we would be separated once more. Maybe all three of us would again be in an orphanage. I disliked the orphanage very badly for there we had no freedom, no contact with people, other than staff. It was like being locked up inside a prison. The sounds of life would be gone, except for the occasional streetcar bell — no trees, no flowers, no blue sky or stars at night.

Worriedly I looked at Edith. She sat on the bed with her hands folded in her lap with quiet tears falling into her lap. Her face and neck showed many blotches of purple and red from the beating Frau Kaiser had given her. With uncertainty in my voice I asked, "What do you think will become of us now?" Her head snapped back and her eyes looked straight at me. I could see that her fight had just begun.

"Tomorrow," she said "we will go to the juvenile authorities and ask to speak to the director in charge of the department."

Chapter 30

Edith never started at the bottom; she always demanded to speak to the top official. Just as she had once asked to speak with the Commander of the Russian army in Prussian Holland in order to ask about the whereabouts of our parents, she now intended to get a hearing from the top official of the juvenile authority.

The next morning, after Frau Kaiser had left for work, Edith shook me by the shoulders told me to get dressed. My morning calm vanished as I remembered the unpleasant incident the day before. I felt lost. The uncertainty of the future ahead, with maybe being sent to a different home without my sisters, to was depressing. Hurriedly we dressed to leave the house, but we could not find our shoes. It was clear that Frau Kaiser had taken our shoes to make sure we could not leave the house, but Edith stated that we did not need shoes to find the Juvenile Department, and that it was even better that way, to say that Frau Kaiser took them away for fear that we might expose her. With that we were on our way to the city office building that wo boliovod hold tho dopartmont.

As we walked into the large grey structure, we saw that there were many several reception offices, each seeming to pertain to different departments. None were labeled "Juvenile Department", so Edith walked into an office at random and asked for directions to it. She was told that it was upstairs on a particular floor, so we walked up a few flights of stairs and there it was: "Juvenile Department of the City of Berlin."

When we entered the reception part of the office, we saw rows and rows of desks occupied by people operating typewriters or talking on telephones. Full of confidence, Edith walked over to the reception desk and asked to speak to the director of the department. When the lady asked about the nature of our visit, Edith explained that she would only discuss the nature of her visit with the director of the department. With that, the lady asked us to follow her and she led us down a long corridor until she came at a door which read "Amtsleiter," or, in English, "Director". We followed her right in.

As we entered the office, the lady explained to the secretary, "These two little girls wish to speak with the director only." The secretary asked us to be seated and disappeared into an adjoining room. When she reappeared, with her in the doorway stood the boss of the department. He was a middle-aged man with dark hair and brown eyes, neatly dressed in a brown suit and tie. He gave us a friendly smile as he motioned us into his office, then invited us to sit down and tell him why we wanted to see him. Edith came right to the point and told him that she wanted to make a complaint against her foster mother, that of mistreatment.

He looked concerned, and asked Edith to tell him about it – and to start at the beginning about how we came to be foster children.

Edith proceeded to describe to him our entire history from past to present. The Amtsleiter listened with intense interest, taking copious notes of what Edith told him, and though this took quite some time, I believe it was about an hour and a half, he let Edith tell him all about it. He interrupted only to ask questions, mainly about details of how we managed to survive for almost a year without parents or any kind of adult supervision. With the youngest of us being only 4 and Edith herself only 11 years old, he stated it was hard to comprehend that all four of us could survive with such difficulties finding food and water, along with not succumbing to the diseases that had killed thousands of people in similar circumstances.

When Edith ended her story, the director stood up and invited us to follow him. We entered another office where he approached a lady clerk sitting at a desk. He handed her his written notes and instructed her to open a case on the matter, and to get any information from us which could be valuable in locating our living relatives, if any.

Edith and I took a seat and the clerk asked us to give her the names of anyone we could remember on both our parents' sides and as much information about their addresses as possible. There were only three that we could come up with, and they were: our grandmother Urte Jakumeit, formerly of Memel, East Prussia; an unmarried sister of our father, Anni Baltuttis, also formerly of Memel; finally, our aunt and uncle, a brother of our father, Ernst Baltuttis and his wife. She was our dear aunt who had gifted us the beautiful doll formerly belonging to her grown daughter, Irma. We knew the full name and that they resided in the city of Leipzig, in the province of Saxony.

With that, our visit was concluded. We were told to go home to our foster parents and not to worry about complications on their part, for the Juvenile Authorities would set up an appointment with them to explain that a search was being conducted to find our relatives.

The search was fruitful, and the Central Children's Welfare Department located two of our father's siblings. On May 30, 1947, they sent off letters to these relatives.

One of our father's sisters, Anni Baltuttis, turned out to be living just on the outskirts of Berlin; she was now married but childless. They were also successful in locating our father's oldest brother, Ernst Baltuttis, in Leipzig. A response to their efforts on our behalf came on July 22, 1947, in which my uncle and his wife stated that they were willing to host the two oldest children; they had room for me in their own home in Leipzig, and had arranged with a family friend to foster Edith, also in Leipzig. Anni Baltuttis, responded and committed to take Waltraut, now 6½ years old, to live in their home.

Here I should explain the reason for the difference in surname spelling between my father's name and his brothers and sisters.

Our family's homeland is the land of Memel, in East Prussia. It was founded in 1252 by the Teutonic Knights, and was settled by Germans from three other regions of Germany: Lübeck; Holstein; and Dortmund. Although it was German for the 693 years from its founding until 1945[12] when it was made a part of Lithuania, its location right next door to Lithuania meant that many ethnic Lithuanians came to live there as well. The 1910 census found that roughly 44% of the population was ethnic Lithuanian (who spoke Lithuanian as their first language), even if they were German citizens. While ethnic Germans predominated in the cities and larger towns, Lithuanians predominated in the rural areas, and there was much intermarriage over the centuries. This resulted in many ethnic German families having Lithuanian-style names, and vice-versa. Our father's family was one of those ethnic German families with Lithuanian-style names.

Lithuanian names tend to end in the letters "-as",

---

[12] With a short break of 19 years after the end of WW I, when first the French and then Lithuania administered the land of Memel.

"-os" and "-is". Our father was born Otto Baltuttis. After he married my mother and joined the German Army, he was asked as a Reichsdeutsche [13] to change his name to eliminate the foreign "-is". This legal action was somewhat costly, but necessary for his service, and his and our surnames became Baltutt. There was some pressure in Memel for Germans with Lithuanian names to change their names as well, but his brothers and sisters never felt sufficient need to do this.

This was why there was this difference between our name and our Baltuttis aunts and uncles.

By the end of our dealings with the officials, I felt incredibly proud of Edith and I admired her immensely. She was strong, determined, and had truly assumed responsibility as our substitute mother. I had always looked to her for the hard decisions that had to be made.

A large part of my admiration of her stemmed from the great contrast between our personalities. I was inhibited, eager to please, and willing to adapt to whatever situation life placed me in. On the other hand, Edith was a rebel, and was determined to make whatever situation she found herself in conform to her will. She was always suspicious and mistrusting, and had inherited the determination and aggression of my mother along with the intelligence of my father.

In school, Edith excelled in every subject. Her work was frequently shown in the display case in the school hall as an example of good work for other children to draw example from. She excelled in art and won first prize in a

---

[13] Reichsdeutsche, literally translated "Germans of the Reich", is an archaic term for those ethnic Germans who resided within the German state that was founded in 1871. In contemporary usage, it referred to German citizens, the word signifying people from the German Reich, i.e., Imperial Germany or Deutsches Reich, which was the official name of Germany between 1871 and 1945.

school competition for drawing a picture of an aquarium. She enjoyed reading the works of such classical writers as the French novelist Émile Zola and the German writer Johann von Goethe, and became interested in Darwin's theory of evolution.

By the time she was 13 years old, she had joined the Youth Group Center in East Berlin. The primary purpose of this establishment was to educate young people about the benefits of life under Communism, but had a secondary purpose of keeping young people off the streets and engaged in healthy recreation. There were musical instruments for children who showed interest in music, and Edith learned to play beginning pieces on both the piano and the guitar. She joined the chess club and played endlessly, night after night. Ping pong tables were also available at the club, and Edith spent many hours practicing the game, playing well enough to win second place in a ping pong tournament for women when she was only 14.

Other activities available through the Youth Group Center included camping, and especially discussion programs of various kinds. Edith loved to ride for miles on the subway to visit other youth group centers to participate in debates, for she was good at this and usually won. She was tenacious and could not be swayed from her opinion once she had made a statement. She was also a realist, and openly approved the good and ridiculed the bad that she saw under Communism. I would have felt it best to be agreeable and only disagree silently, but Edith knew that at her age she had very little or nothing to lose and simply enjoyed being frank in debate.

Many times in the beginning I tagged along with Edith on these youth group events, just for something to do, but if asked for my opinion on something I would shudder. I was shy beyond explanation, and preferred to sit back and let others come up with the answers. In the end, there wasn't much that interested me at the youth group center (I

179

did not care for sports activities or music and hated the silent game of chess), so I stopped showing up. Eventually, I felt that they forgot I existed.

Chapter 31

At the beginning of July 1947, once again I said good-bye to my sisters and to the sad city of East Berlin. My Aunt Else, whom I had never before met, arrived in Berlin to claim Edith and myself as her true relatives. It gave me a much different feeling of belonging, like closer to home. Now I had the privilege of calling them by their rightful titles of "Aunt" and "Uncle," instead of being forced against my will to address strangers with the fictitious titles of "Mother" and "Father."

My Aunt Else was 55 years of age, with hair already white with age, and had a motherly appearance. She was quiet natured and easy going, and her home, in a three-story apartment building, had not been touched by bombs and was elegant and neat. They had three rooms and a large kitchen. In the living room, the traditional sitting room in a German household, was a grand piano on which her daughter Irma practiced her singing lessons.

My cousin Irma was then 27 years old and had the figure of a movie star and a face to match. Her hair was bleached blond and was meticulously coiffured in a glamorous fashion. She had devoted 5 years to the study of music and had daily voice lessons at the piano in her home. She practiced her singing lessons in the coloratura octave for one hour each day. Her voice had a beautiful warm quality and her tunes were flawless and clear. She had already established herself as a professional singer and had had singing engagements in many cities of East Germany. She was now determined to record her songs and to launch her career as a famous singer.

I felt proud to be associated with her name and but was disappointed that my name differed from hers in spelling. Any time my relationship with the up and coming singer Irma Baltuttis came up with new friends at school, I had to explain why my name was not the same as that of my famous cousin.

My Uncle Ernst, the oldest brother of my father, was as close as I could come to keeping the memory of my father alive. In his face I could see my father. He reminded me of him in many ways: he was tall and thin with dark hair combed back just like my father; his eyes were likewise, deep set and blue. I often studied him from a distance and his resemblance to my father made my heart cry out, for I wished so for my father.

But while my Uncle Ernst resembled my father in looks, he was unlike my father in every other way. There were some jarring appearance discrepancies, such as his teeth, which instead of being white and straight, were discolored and uneven. Also, my uncle wore a hearing aid, which gave him a passive appearance. But aside from these, unlike my father's lively personality, he was a man of few words and was only interested in his work as a mechanic and his daily food.

I so wished that he would volunteer stories of my father, but he had little to say, and besides, talking with him was difficult because of his bad hearing and rather ineffective hearing aid. Besides this, he had a stutter, and so rarely engaged in conversation. His questions or answers were always short and direct; then there was silence. As far as their relationship went, my uncle and aunt never argued, and they seemed quiet and balanced.

One day, Irma disclosed to me that she resented her father for a relationship he had had for years with another woman, the woman in fact who had become my sister Edith's foster mother in Leipzig. Without fail, every Sunday afternoon Uncle Ernst would dress up in his only good suit, of navy blue, put on a tie and hat to complete his wardrobe, and then off he would go to visit his lady friend. He would then promptly return each evening to have Sunday dinner with his family.

I could not understand the attraction between these two people. The woman seemed to be about 10 years his junior, but her facial appearance could only be described as grotesque. She was suffering from cancer of the nose, and it had been eaten away by the cancer and showed large holes, and the surrounding skin involving her cheeks and mouth area had been pulled out of proportion by scar tissue.

But her character was such that one could overlook her facial appearance. Her name was Erika Braun, and she was witty, intelligent, and fairly bubbled over with conversation. Her eyes always smiled and she radiated warmth and understanding. She never complained of her facial disfigurement but lived her life looking at the bright side. This was no easy feat, seeing that she had lost her husband in the war, her only child had died of leukemia at the age of 8[14] and she herself had been stricken with cancer that had transformed her face monstrously.

Fortunately, Frau Braun had not lost her home in the war and it remained her castle. She understood how to grow plants of all kinds, and in the summer, she decorated her home with them. Her home also took on her personality in the way of which she displayed paintings of

---

[14] On the ring finger of her left hand she wore a ring in which the two front teeth of her only child were set in gold.

serene landscapes that she had created herself.

Once Edith moved in with her, Erika learned quickly of Edith's distrust and bitterness toward people. She solved this problem by making Edith an equal in her home. So Edith became her companion and friend, not her foster child for whom she felt responsible, and in this demonstration of trust, allowing Edith to have her own opinion, she became her friend and confidant. Edith in her turn became oblivious to Erika's facial disfigurement and only saw her inner beauty.

I am positive that this inner beauty and uniqueness is what attracted my uncle to Erika. According to Edith, his Sunday visits with her were only a meeting of friends. In his soul he felt that if he abandoned such a flower of personality she would surely wilt. So, disregarding the angry looks he received from his daughter Irma, each Sunday afternoon he left for his regular visit. He had assured her that his visits with the woman were nothing but friendship, but still she disapproved. My Aunt Else, however, being of a quiet and reserved nature, seemed to understand and tolerate these visits. She never scolded him or showed jealousy but assumed the position of a wife just the same.

With joy and expectation, I always looked forward to my cousin Irma's return home from the theatrical engagements she had around East Germany. Her return usually meant that she would bring home gifts of vegetables, flowers, and even meat that people presented to her as a token of their admiration. Once she came home and unpacked a large package containing dark, red, bloody meat. She identified it as horse meat and said that it could be marinated to make a delicious sauerbraten. Aunt Else's face lit up with joy when she saw the package of meat, and didn't seem to be bothered at all by the fact that it came from a horse. In those postwar days of shortages and privation, almost nobody turned up their nose just because some meat had come from a horse. At dinner time the next day, everyone praised the tasty meal as fit for a king.

I was very curious about Irma and felt the desire to be close to her whenever she spent time at home. I had an urge to know as much about Irma and show business as I could, such as the glamor, the names of the theaters she performed in, how the audience responded and how much money she earned. In order to get close to Irma to find all this out, I endeavored to do what I could to be invited into her room. The simplest way was to ask her if there were anything I could help her with, and she responded that I could come in and polish her jewelry and shine her shoes. Success!

Once I had been invited into her room, she instructed me on how she cleaned her silver jewelry, which was to use ashes from her cigarettes as a polishing agent. So I began polishing her rings and bracelets until they sparkled like a mirror. I struck up a conversation and found that Irma enjoyed talking. As I was busy polishing the silver pieces, she showed me her whole collection.

There were many beautiful large pieces of costume jewelry that she used for appearance on stage. As a young child bursting with curiosity, I asked to see her gowns and all the glitter which belonged to her profession. Each gown looked lovelier than the one before, and she told me about each gown and the performances she made in each one.

One costume that did not glitter with rhinestones, chiffon or velvet was an old peasant gown that she wore to sing the translated American folk song, "Cotton Fields" by Huddie Ledbetter, which most remember from the words: "When I was a little bitty baby my mama would rock me in my cradle, in the old cotton fields at home." To complete the costume, when performing the song Irma had her face blackened with makeup so as to appear to be an old black woman, and on her head she wore a scarf with black curls protruding from under it. She said it was her most memorable performance.

I found myself longing to be like her, dreaming that someday I could enter a dancing and acting school and learn how to be a performer. I would be admired and applauded by masses of people and become a famous star. I vowed that someday I too would wear elegant gowns just like Irma's.

After I had finished polishing the jewelry and buffing her shoes to a high gloss, she rewarded my efforts with a few East German Marks. The money seemed only paper in my hand for I could not spend it on food, clothes or even candy. The stores carried only items which could be bought with stamps from ration cards. Candy was never seen in stores and clothes could only be sewn by a tailor or seamstress, providing you could bring the material to them.

Irma was approaching the age of 30 but had no steady beau. In the one year I spent with my relatives, I noticed several occasions when she brought home a man friend, a musician, with whom she would spend the night in her room. I was amazed at her boldness and also surprised by her parents allowing such conduct. Nevertheless, her mother often made comments to try to impress upon her that it was high time at her age to consider marriage. Irma rejected this advice, and told her once in an angry tone that she was meant to be an artist and that she was not cut out to be a mother who listened to crying babies or one who tries to please her husband.

In 1947, television had not arrived in Germany, and theater or radio were to be the only entertainment available.

My aunt announced one evening that it was almost time to tune in the radio and listen to Irma's first live performance on the air. Everyone placed themselves close to the radio. My uncle leaned his head as close to the speaker as possible so that the sound could penetrate his hearing aid. The announcer came on and introduced Kurt Henkel's dance orchestra, which was one of East Germany's most famous bands, and they promptly started blasting out the gay melody of a foxtrot. When the music stopped, we all knew Irma's name would be announced.

Then the announcer spoke again, to introduce the new singing star "The charming blond vocalist, Irma Baltuttis." The band played an introduction. Our faces lit up with suspense and Irma's voice came over the air soft and clear. The melody was a tango and the lyrics spoke of love and harmony. When her song ended, no one in the room spoke a word. On her parent's face I could see the pride, and their eyes smiled with approval.

Irma Baltuttis Publicity Photo

Chapter 32

In the short time I was privileged to spend with my Aunt and Uncle, I had the pleasure of taking part on the occasion of Irma reaching her greatest goal – that of becoming a recording star.

Kurt Henkels, one of the famous band leaders of East Germany, had now engaged Irma to record and appear with his dance orchestra. All the rehearsals and recordings were to be made in our city of Leipzig, and often Irma spent many days at the recording studio, rehearsing music for endless hours. On several occasions, my aunt had asked me to take lunch to her.

The first time was quite an experience. When I arrived at the building, I walked down a long hallway until I found a door with a sign that read "Kurt Henkels Recording Studio." Outside the door was a lighted sign read that indicated "Quiet Please," and I could hear the band playing inside. Not knowing how to make myself noticeable enough to be invited inside, I waited. When the music stopped, I decided to ignore the sign and just walked in.

I found the musicians seated in a half circle – there must have been 15 of them – and I noticed my cousin Irma standing enclosed in a glass chamber. And there was Kurt Henkels himself positioned in the middle of the room from where he directed the proceedings. He did see me, but said nothing and just motioned me to take a seat. He then gave the sign and the band started again.

In my ears, the music sounded unbearably loud. The sound waves seemed to vibrate everything inside me. All over the floor I noticed heavy electric cables. Now for the first time, I had met in person with the famous dance band and its leader, Kurt Henkels. The band played and Irma sang inside her glass chamber until the piece was done, then the music stopped again. When the music ceased, I felt a numbness in my ears and had the sensation of swaying. Irma exited the booth, walked over to me, took her lunch out of my hand and patted me on the head. She then said something to me that I could not hear and escorted me out of the studio.

I was ecstatic. Never in my life had I been so near to famous show people. It hit me then that my cousin Irma was a star and I lived in her house! If only my name had had that "-is" annexed to its end – then my friends at school would not doubt my story when I told them that Irma Baltuttis was my cousin.

I became very enchanted with show business. Looking through a book of show people, I studied their faces and read everything about them. Secretly, I wanted to become a movie star, go to acting school, and take dancing lessons. I dared not ask how to begin entering show business for fear that I might be told that I had no talent or that I was not pretty enough or just be laughed at. I cut out a picture of a German movie star, Marica Rock, who happened to be the prettiest of all the others in my opinion. I made up a passport, pasted her picture to it and pretended from then on that I was the movie star. In school, I revealed my secret to my best girlfriend, Christa, and she too became a beautiful movie star named Zara Leander.

On many afternoons Christa and I stepped into our

imaginary characters and transformed ourselves into being rich and famous, adored and thought of as movie stars. The open meadow became our estate, the clump of trees our homes, and the tree stump became our Rolls Royce. It is easy to pretend when one is a child. The mind can take on an unreal destiny and actually live in it for a time, but only for a time. It can become painful to wake up and step back into reality.

As time passed by, the longing for my parents became stronger. I felt the emotional need of their touch. I longed to use the title "mother." I felt hurt inside when other children used the words "my mother" in conversations, and my life seemed empty and lonely. My thoughts more often regressed into the past, where I could stare into space and see my home with my mother and sisters, and my father always coming home on weekends. It was a sweet dream from which I hated to wake up. If there only could be a way to have them back – but there was none.

Often, as I walked to school, my mind would spontaneously wander off to Osterode, East Prussia. I would find myself on the sand hills, with warm winds blowing in my face. I tried often to put my mind into that state purposely, but the harder I tried, the less I succeeded. It seemed to happen involuntarily at quiet moments, when I sat in my classes or walked to and from school. This mind wandering was the only way I could turn back the time. It became my sweetest moment. Often my teacher would call out my name and shout, "Rita, stop daydreaming and pay attention in this class!" I would shudder and my face would become flushed. I was embarrassed for I would have no idea what the topic was.

The only solution for my constant longing was to pray I remembered everything that my grandmother had taught me about prayer, that it is to be heard by God our Father. I especially remembered in my prayers, "not to be greedy." It became a nightly habit. As I lay in my bed in the darkened room, my mind always tried to wander home, and so I prayed, "My dear God, my heart is so heavy from hurt that my message to you has to pass through all the voices that are praying to you now. Asking for all the joy and happiness on earth would be greedy of me. Take my father if you have to make a choice, but please give us the one we need most, our mother. Lord, I need to use the word 'mother.' I need her to comb my hair and wash my clothes. I need her to hold on to."

Even though the love for my father exceeded that for my mother, I needed her desperately. I fabricated images of my parents in my mind, and they were always alive. I could see then in the mirror of my mind. They talked to me, smiled, and nodded. In the realm of my fantasy, I could see again my father stepping back as if he approved of my choosing mother over him. As I pleaded with God and prayed that I was willing to sacrifice my father to have my mother, I felt guilty. I sometimes cried myself to sleep asking my father to forgive me. Living under the burden of this emotional stress and lack of sleep became detrimental to my health. I lost more weight so that my ribs could be visibly counted. My face was pale and I started failing in my classes.

Chapter 33

In early summer of 1948, I was again selected to spend six glorious weeks of summer on a farm in the province of Mecklenburg. Although I had never taken ill and felt physically healthy, in appearance I remained frail and sickly. The light blond hair against my thin pale face and my tiny boned body frame was a great advantage to me, for it always made it possible for me to be eligible for a summer vacation on a farm.

This time, I was placed with a family which had children of their own. They were all girls of school age. Their home was modest, somewhat rumpled, and unkempt in appearance, but they were very hard working. Everything was done manually. Oxen helped plow the fields, weeds had to be eradicated by hoes. Cows were milked by hand and potatoes were also harvested by the family and gathered in baskets. The household was a busy factory from dawn to dusk.

I spent time helping the girls in the kitchen. I would entertain them with stories of my life in East Prussia, telling of my life in Berlin of foster parents and the orphan home I so disliked. The girls would listen in disbelief. They had never spent time away from their parents or their farm. The war had had little impact on these people and their lives remained the same as it had been before and during the war. The girls wanted to know all about the beautiful city of Berlin, about which they had studied in school. Their impression was that Berlin was a city of glitter and glamour with film stars and theaters. When I told them that Berlin laid in ruins and that many people made their homes in them for lack of housing, that they lived on meager rations of food, even the water and electricity was rationed and people died every day of hunger, they told me that had to be making it up.

There was life in that household and I enjoyed the company of the girls, all young and imaginative. I followed them around gathering eggs from their chickens and watched the ducks swim in their pond and helped feed the cattle. I would walk with them as we explored the fields.

In the evening, the time was spent for each one as they pleased. Often we sat huddled together in darkness telling sinister stories of ghosts and monsters. For a moment, like a wave, their companionship helped to wash away the agony of my craving. My thoughts became geared to socializing with the daughters of my farm family and plunging my senses into the warm, blue, sunny days of summer.

Farm life is a carefree life. It is as close to nature as one can get. As far as the eyes can see between the horizon and the earth a multitude of colors stretch like a carpet across the land. Interrupting tranquility is a bird, carefree and chirping in flight. No, I thought, war had never touched this part of my country. People in this part of the land cannot comprehend the explosions of bombs, the Russian soldiers setting fire to their homes. They did not have to pack their bare necessities and flee their homes not knowing if ever they would see the morning sun. I envisioned that when I was grown, I too would find a place of serenity, a place on earth where no one could touch me, away from the turmoil of industry, big cities and people, where only forests and open fields surrounded my life.

Two weeks before my departure from my farm friends, I was handed a letter. It was very unusual to receive mail of any kind, especially for me. The envelope bore the address of my Aunt Else in Leipzig. Everyone seemed excited and stood waiting for me to open my mail. Wanting to share the excitement with everyone, I read the contents out loud.

"Dear Rita, we are happy for you that you had been chosen to spend the summer on a farm. Being surrounded by the young girls will make your stay more pleasant. It will be a joy to see you again with rosy cheeks and your weight increased." Finally, she closed with these words: "Fate has been cruel to you, but you know you must always hope. It could very well be that your mother will soon return."

I ended up reading that last sentence over and over. Why would she suddenly mention my mother? Never before had she discussed my parents, always carefully avoiding the issue. The very scope of my existence had been hoping and waiting. Were my prayers to the Lord going to be answered? I did not know how to act or what to do next. I felt breathless with excitement and started pacing the room like an impatient animal. I walked out to the farm yard, sat on a fence post, and prayed.

"Oh dear God," I told Him, "please let it be true. Bring my mother to me when I return. Please dear Lord, don't forsake me in my hopes for I cannot bear it. Please let it be so. I have waited 3½ years for this and now only 14 days remain. I must wait."

How will she look and what will she say? I visualized tears in my mother's eyes as she held me in her arms. I thought, I will make up to her the suffering she had to endure. I will love and honor her until the day she dies. At home in our park, I will break off a big bouquet of roses

and present them to her every day they are in bloom. Oh, if I could only go home now. But what if my Aunt had made an empty statement, only wishing it could be so? No, I thought, she would not write and include a statement referring to my mother without a cause. She was too considerate for that.

The remaining days became dreams of joy. I visualized being together with all my sisters again, stroking my mother's dark hair, kissing her cheeks, and most of all, I would use the word, "mother" in every sentence of my conversation. She will love me and hold me. She will cook my food and comb my hair. I will walk with her and hold her hand. She will never leave again.

My farm friends were taking part in my joy, but cautiously, and said I must not react too positively, for my aunt had not actually written that she *was* home but that she *could* be home. But I disregarded their suggestions and continued to be filled with hope. I never ceased to believe that my prayers had been answered. Impatiently, I counted the days before I was able to return, and like an animal tied to a chain, I struggled with my emotions, trying to keep them from breaking loose to run as fast as my legs would carry me into the arms of my long, lost mother.

Chapter 34

Finally, the day of my departure had come. Feverishly, I threw my belongings into my suitcase, watched the clock, and roamed back and forth from the house to the dusty country road in hopes of seeing the arrival of the truck which would carry our group to the train station. As the truck pulled in, I thanked my friends for their wonderful hospitality and promised that I would write and tell them of my reunion with my mother. They smiled and we said good-bye.

In the truck, I took a seat among other very happy children who were departing with the anticipation of being back again in the secure loving homes of their parents. Like a choir, they turned to singing a folk song, had merry conversations, and giggled. Myself, I could not participate in their fun, for my mind was filled with thoughts of a new future with my mother and sisters.

After long hours of traveling, the train arrived in Leipzig. Stretching my neck to find a familiar face, I discovered my aunt and uncle both. My uncle, dressed in his best suit, discovered me as I waved to him from the window. I grabbed my suitcase and squeezed myself through all the laughing and squealing children toward the exit. As I greeted my guardians, they smiled happily at me.

Immediately, I brought up the letter which Aunt Else had written, asking about my mother and wanting to hear all the details. She nodded her head, and proceeded with the welcome news, that yes, my mother had indeed returned, and that she was waiting for me in Berlin with my sisters!

She went on to fill me in on everything she knew about what had happened, that mother had been in a forced labor camp in the Ural Mountains in Russia until just recently when the Soviets had released her and many others to return home to Germany. That when arrived back in Germany she was first placed in a homecoming and quarantine camp for returning prisoners of war in Frankfurt an der Oder in East Germany. There she had given the Red Cross search service the names and possible locations of family members, and had waited for news of where they might be, especially her children, whom she hadn't known would be alive.

As she explained all the details, my emotions became so intense, it was difficult to hold back the tears of longing and pain. I cried out. Silently, my relatives walked me home, and within two days I found myself back in Berlin. It was August 1948. I was now almost 12 years old, with my birthday coming up in the next month.

My aunt and I arrived at the train station and immediately boarded a street car that was heading in the correct direction. Along the way we passed a great deal of activity. The city of Berlin still looked cluttered with ruins, with many people still busy working to clear the rubble with the aid of wheelbarrows. Women young and old were working with chisels to clean off the bricks, trucks were carrying away the dusty rubble, and in some places, foundations were being poured for new buildings. The city was noisy and everybody in the city seemed to be at work rebuilding.

After changing streetcar routes several times, we got off at the stop closest to the address my aunt had been given of where my mother was living, and started walking. After a short walk we came up to a small grey apartment building that matched the address and Aunt Else said "This is the house!" We were looking for an apartment on the ground floor, and without knocking we walked right through the door.

With great anticipation, I sought for mother, to see her face; instead, there was Edith. She came toward us and with a happy smile she put her arms around my neck and kissed me on the mouth. Next, I noticed my youngest sister, Waltraut, as she sat timidly on a burlap sack that was stuffed with straw. And there was my sister Irmgard, smiling her biggest smile showing off her big dimples. She happily shouted for me to look at what she could do, and she made a handstand on a roughly boarded wall.

I turned to Edith and asked why our mother was not here and where she was. Edith shrugged her shoulders.

"Mother is at the government housing office trying to have this dreary little room officially awarded to us as so-called housing. Don't worry, you'll see her soon. She said that she would be home before evening."

Upon hearing this, Aunt Else nodded and told us that since she was in town she would take advantage of the opportunity to visit with her brother, who lived in West Berlin. She said she would return to the apartment before departing for home. And so she left.

I looked around at the four walls and could barely envision that this place was our home. It was unfurnished, with several burlap sacks stacked on the floor for sitting and sleeping upon. In the corner stood a gas stove. The sole window in the room was bare and the view depressing. Out the window, as far as I could see, were buildings marred by bombs, burned and hollow, and walls with the mortar cracked off and the bricks exposed. On some buildings, their whole fronts were missing with their bricks crumbled into heaps.

The only evidence of our mother's presence was a metal plate and associated eating utensils, such as fork, knife, and spoon. When I asked Edith to tell me about our mother, her attitude was somewhat negative. She said I should wait and would see her soon.

This room had been part of a three-room apartment that was partitioned into a two-family dwelling. In the other two rooms on the other side of the boarded wall there lived a young widow with her five small boys. She had the privilege of a kitchen to herself, for she had occupied the apartment before us. It was like night versus day compared to my former home with our Aunt and Uncle. "This isn't a home," I thought, "but a naked shelter without beds, and without even a table and a chair to sit on!" We had a stove to cook food, but no dishes to eat on. These four walls called living quarters were utterly distressing. But, at last, I was home.

When I jokingly asked Irmgard if she liked this place, Irmgard smiled and told me that we wouldn't have to worry about her, for she could always stay with her foster parents.

It was late afternoon and Edith and I were seated on the wide windowsill, which, except for burlap sacks on the floor, offered the only place to sit. We discussed my stay on the farm and in turn Edith told of Erika Braun and how much she would miss seeing her. Then the door opened and there in the doorway stood my dear mother.

In silence my senses reached out to her and consumed her whole being. Her hair was short and straight, her face looked the same as I remembered, but somewhat coarser. Her dress was blue and white striped, and reminded me of prison clothes. On her feet she wore black shoes, the kind that soldiers wear as dress shoes.

As she walked toward me with her arms stretched

out, I stood up. We put our arms around each other, then she knelt down and with tears in her eyes she looked up into my face and said, "Unlike your sisters, you have not grown much." She held me tighter and did not speak anymore. I was trying to hold back my tears and not let my emotions run away from me, and I managed to whisper, "Mother, I have waited so long." My face was buried in her bosom. I could barely catch my breath. For a moment, I wondered if this was only be a dream. But here before me I held my mother!

She led me to the windowsill where we sat together and she proceeded to tell of the struggle she was having, fighting with the city housing authority for the right to stay in this very room, which was only loaned to us on a temporary basis. The government had so far repeatedly denied her a residence permit for the city of Berlin, because they had an endless list of people waiting to be assigned any kind of decent housing. So she had been returning to the Housing Authority offices over and over again, waiting there until her name was called, only to hear them again deny her appeal for this small room in which we all had found happiness. Then she would put in another appeal and repeat the process yet again.

With tears running down her cheeks, she shook her head no and said that it didn't matter, for she would fight to stay in Berlin. This was where our life had come together and this was where we would make our home – and in this very room!

"I have survived 3 1/2 years of hard labor in Russia and have managed to exist and live for the day of my release. Now that I have found what is left of my life, I will never cease to struggle to make a life for us, together."

Right then I wanted to ask my mother about Russia but felt inhibited because of the emotional turmoil I found myself in, and decided to save it until a later date. The words would not escape from my throat.

That day will remain the most unforgettable and emotional event in my life. I have no other memory or details as far as what kind of food we ate that evening if any. Aunt Else must have come back to the apartment before departing back to Leipzig, but I don't remember that, either. At the end of the day, I laid my head on my burlap bed and felt calmness, indescribable joy, and peace. As if a stone had been lifted from my heavy heart, I loved even the bare walls and my burlap bed. There in the shadows lay my mother! Was she asleep, I wondered? Tomorrow I will be calm and I will say, "Mother, please don't stay so long at the city offices. No more foster homes, no more orphan homes. Now I belong to you forever. I am home!"

I lay awake wondering what I could do for my mother. It was summertime, maybe I could find flowers? Roses, I thought would be perfect for her for they are the flowers of love. Then I fell asleep.

Chapter 35

When I awoke the next morning, the sun was shining bright through our window. I looked over to my mother's bed on the floor. It was empty. I was disappointed but not sad, for I knew she would be back. Did she give me a kiss good-bye, I wondered? I wished that I had not been asleep when she left. I could have said, "Good-bye mother, come back soon!"

Soon, Edith stirred on her burlap sack on the floor. She lifted her head, face looking sweaty and red with the pattern of the burlap imprinted on it. Sleepily, she smiled.

"Is mother gone?" she asked.

I nodded my head yes. I could hardly wait until she was home again. Edith got up and walked toward the stove. Here was some bread and two potatoes.

"We should borrow a kettle from Frau Günther next door and make some soup," she said.

"How can we make soup with only two potatoes?" I wondered. Edith said that two potatoes could make enough soup for all of us. She and I walked to the other apartment and asked to borrow a kettle. The lady, Frau Günther, was young. She had blond hair, blue eyes, and a welcoming smile. She would have been very attractive if it had not been for her eyes which looked extremely crossed. Looking at her, I could not be sure whether her attention was directed at Edith or myself. During the visit her five small boys continued to jump wildly around the room, while a baby cried hysterically in his crib. Her room was not as sparse as ours; she owned three metal beds, complete with pillows and blankets. By her window stood a table and several chairs. There was bread and sugar on the table and several cups and spoons.

As we were engaged in the conversation, she busied herself by wetting the bread and sprinkling it with sugar. Seeing this, one of her little blue-eyed, blond boys would come running hungrily and grab for it. She did not offer any to us, instead she led us into the kitchen and handed us her kettle. With a smile she said for us not to hesitate to ask for utensils, and she was glad to share with us until our mother was able to accumulate these needed items for herself. We thanked her and walked back to our room.

Edith and I busied ourselves over the stove to make the soup with two potatoes. Without peeling them, Edith ground the potatoes in a potato grinder while she boiled salted water in the kettle. Once the water came to a boil she carefully poured the finely ground potatoes into the salted water, stirring in order to prevent lumps from forming. It cooked very quickly became thick and soon the soup was ready to eat. With a slice of bread each, we ate our meal. If our mother managed to bring home some food tonight, there would be some more tomorrow; if not, there would be none.

My youngest sister, Waltraut, seemed very quiet sitting on her straw bed. She was now 7½ years old. Making conversation with her for the first time since I had arrived the day before, I asked how she had liked staying with our father's sister, Aunt Anny. She stated that Aunt Anny had never been nice to her and that she was glad to be no longer with her. Waltraut had had a problem with bedwetting that Aunt Anny had punished her many times about. First, she was made to stand in the corner with her face against the wall. When this failed to correct the problem, Aunt Anny spanked her with a whip. After that, Waltraut said that she had tried to stay awake all night so that she was awake to use the washroom. Exhausted, she fell asleep and to her horror, she discovered in the morning that the bed was wet again. Aunt Anny became violent and spanked her again. She used language to embarrass Waltraut, calling her a lazy little pig and rubbed her face into the wet sheets.

Waltraut had become quite shy of people. She very seldom played with little girls her age, and was by preference silent. She liked to spend her time looking at picture books, and as she became older and mastered reading she surrounded herself with books and could spend days reading. Because of this we affectionately used the nickname *Leseratte*[15] for her. This is the equivalent of the English term "Bookworm".

The morning after I was reunited with Mother, Irmgard had awakened with a bright smile and said that she would be going home now. She said she would try to return that afternoon, but if she was not there not to worry for she would be home with her mom (she called her foster parents mom and dad). She felt very much at home with these people and she loved them. They had made Irmgard feel as if she were the daughter they had wished for all their lives.

The first contact my mother made as she arrived in Berlin had been with Herr and Frau Bach. They had received the joyous and shocking news from the German Red Cross that our mother had returned from Russia and were given her arrival schedule in Berlin. Frau Bach now knew that she had to give Irmgard back to her rightful mother.

---

[15] "Reading rat".

When we became separated from our parents on February 13, 1945, Irmgard was just past her fifth birthday. The impact of missing her mother and being dependent upon her two older sisters for her survival had great impact upon her emotional state. She cried because of her missing her mother; that and events like Edith having to shave off her pretty thick hair to rid it of lice, were just a couple of the great negative events that she had had to bear at such a young age.

When she was placed with Frau Bach, this gave her a real home for the first time in nearly a year, which for a six year old was a large portion of her life to that point. In order to come to terms with all the dislocations, she appeared to have blanked out anything about having another mother somewhere. The memory of her real mother faded away over the years while her foster parents raised her with genuine love and caring. She could not break that tie when her real mother did finally appear, since she had had Frau Bach as her loving mother for almost half her life.

Although certainly dismayed to find that she might have to give Irmgard up as her loving daughter, nevertheless Frau Bach took it in good heart and made plans to receive Irmgard's mother as if she were royalty. She started to scrimp on her ration card and saved enough to bake a cake for her arrival. Out of bed sheet, she had sewn a pleated skirt for Irmgard and also a pink blouse. Finally she had arranged Irmgard's hair in long, beautiful corkscrew curls with a white ribbon tied in back.

Before leaving to meet our mother, Frau Bach purchased a large bouquet of roses and off they went to the Anhalter Bahnhof[16]. The station was packed with people waiting for returnees, and with those who were returning

---

[16] The Anhalter Bahnhof (Anhalter Train Station) was at that time the Berlin arrival point for returnees from Russian capitivity.

from captivity, as well as regular travelers from other points. Many of those waiting wiped their eyes in anticipation of greeting their loved ones for the first time after many years of hoping. Others, stood waiting just hoping that maybe out of all the returnees, among them was their son, daughter, or lost husband, or even someone who knew something about their fate. Often women held up signs with pictures of their loved ones on which was written such things as "Does anyone know my son Heinz Krüger?" The sign would state when he was born and when he was captured.

Nurses from the Red Cross stood by each box car as the train arrived, ready to give assistance. As she got off the train, my mother was anxiously looking for her four little girls who she had been told would be there to meet her, but could not find any that looked like hers. Searching all the faces, her eyes became glued to the pretty little girl dressed in white and pink holding a bouquet of roses.

As she slowly approached the little girl with the flowers, she studied her until she recognized her own daughter standing before her. She asked, "What is your name, little girl?" Irmgard studied the lady with her big blue eyes, not recognizing her as her mother and said, "My name is Irmgard Baltutt." Kneeling down to her, my mother then took her by the shoulders and in joy she cried, "I am your mother! Do you remember me? I am your mother!" Irmgard's eyes filled with tears and she stretched out her arms to hand her the roses, and they held each other.

After a few moments, Frau Bach interrupted this reunion to introduce herself as Irmgard's guardian. At mother's query as to why her other three daughters were not on hand – the Red Cross had told her that they were all in Berlin, information which had become obsolete – Frau Bach explained that they could not be present for they were not after all in Berlin, and had not yet been notified.

From the start, Frau Bach took my mother into her home, rather than have her stay in the crowded temporary quarters that the authorities provided returnees. She treated her royally and tried to help melt the ice between Irmgard and her real mother, who had failed to recognize her.

In fact, Frau Bach really went out of her way to be helpful in all of my mother's efforts to settle in Berlin. When Edith came rushing to Berlin from Leipzig upon news of mother's return, and after Waltraut was gathered in from our Aunt Anny's in the village of Grossziethen just outside Berlin, Frau Bach made room in her home for all of us, until my mother could be given a place of her own. This didn't take long for soon after mother had registered in Berlin as a released prisoner, she was given consideration and placed in temporary housing. In fact, this was the very room of my reunion with her, complete with a stove and five burlap sacks filled with straw for sleeping.

As my mother struggled to be awarded residence in Berlin and also keep the room which first provided a roof over our heads, Irmgard stayed in the loving arms and home of her foster mother. She stayed away longer each time. First, overnight, and then a week and longer. Mother permitted it because she had the thought that why should Irmgard have to suffer all our privations, too, for no good reason, when she had a much more pleasant place to live. She eventually regretted this decision, since it led to a continuing estrangement between her and Irmgard.

That evening, mother arrived home late. She looked so very distressed in her drab blue and white dress with men's shoes on her feet. The Red Cross has given her the dress and shoes on the day of her discharge from the quarantine camp. The dress was now wrinkled, its hem line extended far below her knees and it reminded me of prison garb. Why must she still look like she is a prisoner?

After all, I thought, she is free now. But I wanted to reach out to her and tell her it didn't matter. All I cared about was that she was home.

Mother sat on the windowsill, her face flushed and a glint of triumph in her eyes.

"I have good news," she announced. "After all the tears I've shed and the countless hours I spent talking to one official after another has finally paid off: we've finally been granted residence in Berlin!"

This meant that the room we were now occupying would be our permanent home. And while it wasn't much to look at, at least it was a roof over our heads. Additionally, mother was eligible for ration cards and a monthly allowance of 35 Marks for each child and 100 for herself, to help pay for incidental needs. Official residence also conferred the right to be given work and all the other considerations that were available to residents.

Edith ran up to mother and hugged her neck and said, "I am like you, Mother, I never give up until I get what I ask for. I took your place when you and father were taken from us, and I fought back when people mistreated my sisters and myself. I walked to the Russian headquarters and complained about Herr Klein who had beaten me with his cane and separated me from my sisters." Mother's eyes filled with tears and with both hands she stroked Edith's cheeks and whispered "little mother."

Chapter 36

The hot summer of 1948 came to an end. September arrived, with it my twelfth birthday, and of course school was about to start. Again, I entered another strange school where everyone was unknown to me.

During the war, hospitals, children's homes and most schools had been marked with illuminated signs on their roofs showing a red cross for enemy planes to recognize them and perhaps avoid their destruction. My school was one of those, a large grey building that had been spared from the bombs.

The curriculum at the school made it mandatory for every student to study the Russian language, and a student who failed in that one subject would fall behind a whole year. But Russian was important for practical reasons, since we were in the Soviet sector of Berlin, as there were thousands of Russian-speaking troops and officials.

Our Russian teacher was a pretty young woman with dark, curly hair and a bright smile. She was very even-tempered, but didn't control her classroom very well. Frequently when she entered the classroom, the children would start being unruly, yelling "stay out!" Disregarding their rudeness, she would enter the class with her brightest smile, step up to the podium and order silence.

209

Reluctantly, the class would then come to order and we would proceed with our lessons. On many occasions when the class could not be settled down by our even-tempered teacher, she would pull out a story book and read the most enchanting fairy tales about peasants, kings, and firebirds, stories always of Russian origin. The class would then sit in utter silence as she read from the book, not wishing to interrupt, for the stories were better than Grimm's fairy tales by far.

A second language could be chosen if one desired, of which Spanish or English were the available choices. Everyone in my class chose who chose a second language chose to learn English, including me. Of course, the English language was easier for Germans to learn because it had the same Latin alphabet, and it is also a Germanic language. While on the other hand, the Russian language belongs to the Slavic branch and its Cyrillic alphabet is difficult, or at least it was that way for me.

My English teacher was also my homeroom teacher, and he, unlike the Russian teacher, demanded respect and had full control over his class. In those days, a teacher guided the same children from the first to the eighth grade until everyone branched off to a vocational school of their choice. A homeroom teacher became a parent substitute, knowing everything about every child, their strengths and weaknesses and had the authority to physically punish a child or for that matter, mentally abuse one by ordering him to stand in the corner facing the wall. Arriving late to school was utterly unacceptable, and if one were tardy it would result in being lectured on the subject of "What effect tardiness may have in adulthood when one was employed," or how "a tardy person is regarded as irresponsible."

In the Soviet Zone, history was taught with a decidedly pro-Communist slant. They ignored the subject of Hitler and the Second World War, and it was never explained to me why Germany fought many nations or why

Hitler rounded up millions of Jews to exterminate them in his concentration camps. Instead, we were taught about how Communism was the best way of life and superior to Capitalism. However, this was the wrong place to try to teach this kind of thing. Children living in Berlin could freely roam between the Western and Eastern sectors of their city and see for themselves.

The American sector of Berlin had stores filled with food, with store windows displaying foreign fruits such as bananas, oranges, and pineapples. Also on sale were coffee beans, pastries and chocolates, all the goodies one could desire. Movie theaters showed American western movies and musicals. Neon signs brightened up the city and the streets smelled of prosperity. Clothing stores stocked the latest of Western fashion. The black market openly flourished, and sidewalk peddlers offered to exchange 1 West Mark for 7 East Marks or vice versa. American cigarettes, with "Pall Mall" being the most popular brand, could be bought for 20 West Marks or 140 East Marks. One chocolate could be bought for 1 West Marks or 7 East Marks. I had not tasted candy of any kind or had eaten an orange or tasted good chocolate in years. Looking in the display windows, I wished very much that I too could have access to such splendor.

In contrast to the American sector, the Soviet Sector was overwhelmingly dull. No neon lights brightened the city, and the facades of stores looked plain, and almost shabby. The only advertising in stores were windows that were painted with white chalk to inform people what kind of food was available and how many food stamps were required to obtain any. Shoes could only be bought by applying to the Department of Textiles, and were rationed: the limit was one pair of shoes for each member of the family once per year. And such shoes! They consisted of burlap uppers with wooden soles. In order to obtain rationed meat or lard, one had to wait in a long line outside the meat store, and only when the commodity was available. In our history class, we were taught of the Communist- inspired five-year plan, and how the German people could look forward to a brighter future under the leadership of Walter Ulbricht[17]. When my teacher preached this doctrine to us, a bright boy in class questioned what he was teaching, and pointed out the contrast he was exposed to, namely the relative abundance and obtainability of food and clothing in West Berlin, as compared to what we saw in the East. "Why," he asked, "can't we have the same kind of life?"

Our teacher, Herr Schönfeld, not being in a position to honestly give his personal views on politics, had to maintain the assigned topic of the five-year plan. He could not answer the question.

Myself, I never participated in any kind of discussion because I felt inadequate about talking in front of others. If I happened to get called upon in class, my face would become flushed and I would feel like I could hardly say a word. For this reason I always purposely selected the seat in class which I best judged to make me invisible to the teacher; this was usually toward the back, in the middle of the row. There, I could hide behind all the eager-to-talk students and daydream.

This was very much unlike my sister Edith, who applied herself in every subject including sports activities, led her class with perfect grades, and always participated in class discussions. She was looked upon by her classmates as a leader, while I kept to myself, and got average grades. I was always frail, underweight, and shorter than other girls my age. I was never included in the popular circle of girls who told each other secrets and giggled over boys.

Secretly, I entertained thoughts of immigrating to

---

[17] Walter Ulbricht was the General Secretary of the Socialist Unity Party in East Germany from 1950 to 1973, and the actual leader of the country.

America when I reached adulthood. I had heard from other children, who had relatives in the United States of America, that there were households who owned one or even two cars. They worked and had maids to keep their houses. There, I thought, I could eat all the chocolate candy and bananas I wanted. I would find work, wear nice clothes, and maybe even buy a car. So I was eager to learn the English language.

I studied my lessons well and practiced seriously in my English book, *A Lady Gallops Around the Arena on a White Horse*. My book showed a picture of a circus arena with a lady all dressed in glitter doing acrobatics on the back of a white horse. I repeated the sentence over and over. It sounded so beautifully foreign and I could read and sound out the words so fluently I wanted to learn English more than anything else.

Chapter 37

I was punished only once during my school years.

It was customary in Germany to show respect for one's teacher as he or she entered the room, which meant we were required to stand up in greeting, and remain standing until we were told we could sit down. So, as usual one morning I was sitting at my desk, when the teacher entered the classroom. After he asked us to be seated, he busied himself at the podium calling the roll. My name Baltutt meant that I was second on his list, and then there were ten wasted minutes while he called the rest of the 45 names.

I was hungry, and as he unhurriedly read them out one by one, mainly looking at his list, I felt he would not notice if I took a bite of the only sandwich I had for the day. Now, it was strictly against the rules to eat in class during sessions, and a lunch period was set aside for that purpose. So I carefully took one bite and then another until I had eaten it all. It seemed like I had gotten away with this, since he did not interrupt his roll-calling until he was done.

But after he was finished, Herr Schönfeld calmly closed the cover of his list, looked straight at me and ordered me up to the front of the class. When I arrived at the podium, he stood up from his chair, held out his right arm and his hard hand landed on my cheek. The impact on my face had such force that it made me very dizzy. As I stood there stunned, with blurred vision, he warned me that I must never eat during class again and then ordered me back to my seat. In that moment I could not see clearly enough to do that, but nevertheless I made my way, stumbling as I went.

I tried not to show my hurt by crying. Instead, I tried to act as calm as I could possibly manage. My face felt like it was on fire, my ear throbbed and ached, and my heart pounded in my chest. All eyes were now turned toward me. I could barely cope with the embarrassment. Back in my seat I huddled in on myself, feeling low, and I thought of revenge. What could I do about this, I wondered? It quickly occurred to me that I would tell my mother. She would then go to the principal and complain that I had been injured in the ear. Herr Schönfeld would surely then apologize to me.

As I went home that afternoon I thought it was the first time I felt I could lean on my mother. She would take me in her arms and stroke my face, I thought. How good it was that now I had my very own mother to lean on! But when I eagerly told my mother that I had been struck by my teacher, she did not take me in her arms or stroke my face but took his side. She told me that the teacher expected discipline from every child and that I had been punished justly. She explained that in her schooldays teachers punished children even worse by using a whip or would strike their hands with a ruler.

I was disappointed in her attitude and said no more. There had always been a traditional distance between any teacher and a class: respect was demanded and no one dared to argue. But after this experience, whatever respect I might have had for my teacher had turned into fear.

This fear prevented me from trying to resolve the problem of hungry children trying to steal each other's food when we were out of the classroom, such as when we were at the gym. Often I would return to class only to find that someone had taken my only sandwich – so I would have nothing to eat that day. Although I tried to prevent this by leaving last or returning ahead of everyone else, this didn't stop it. Telling the teacher might have helped, but I could never report the theft; my relationship with the teacher had been broken permanently.

I disregarded most of my subjects as unimportant but studied English feverishly, both in and out of school. Walking home from school I began building sentences with the new words I had learned that day. It wasn't long before I had mastered a small but respectable vocabulary.

I had gotten permission from Frau Gunther to use her radio when she wasn't at home, and on those occasions and as soon as I arrived home, I felt driven to listen to it, tuning it to the United States Armed Forces Network. Of course it was broadcast in English.

I wanted so much to learn and understand more than we were taught in school. To me the English language had a pleasant sound, and I listened avidly as the announcer's words rolled soft and smooth from his lips. American music also had a ring of excitement for me, and as I listened to its rhythms my body felt compelled to sway as if I were dancing. No other music in the world had the quality and the beat of American music. I desired to understand their lyrics; I wanted to know the whole story of J.A. Staffords', "You Belong to me," or Frankie Lane's "Jezebel." Listening to my favorite sounds, my dreams carried me across the ocean. I visualized the skyscrapers, bright neon lights, store windows full of the latest fashions and the marketplaces laden with food and candy.

Yes, I thought, someday I want to go there. In America, there were no ruins, the land had not been bombarded in the war, and people talked of the United States as if it were a fairyland – "the land of milk and honey" and "the great land of opportunity and millionaires." Some of the sidewalks in New York City were paved with silver coins, it was said.

I felt unrest clawing at my soul, like a bird locked away trying to spread its wings in flight, only to be bounced back by the wires of its cage. "East Berlin," I thought, "You are my enemy. You have nothing to offer me but degradation – like the need to become a thief in the night stealing fruit from trees in the summer, which is practically the only way to get them, or the need to steal coal for warmth in the winter."

Chapter 38

One evening I was lost in my dreams as the mother of darkness spread her wings over the barren room which was my home and the radio was playing "Your Cheating Heart." When I heard a loud knock at the door, I tuned off the radio and hurried to answer.

In the doorway stood two middle aged men, both well-dressed in suits and ties. They identified themselves as being from a church mission, so I invited them in and asked the nature of their visit. The older one spoke and said that they were there to look after people in extreme need, in which category we seemed to fall. He continued on to say that my mother had appeared to the church mission to be need of the bare necessities for herself and her children to sustain life.

They proceeded to ask me many questions about our family, such as the ages of all us children and how many years mother had spent in the labor camps in the Ural Mountains. The younger of the two men wanted to know if my mother owned a winter coat? I shook my head no. They stood in silence as their eyes wandered to every corner of the room.

One of the men scribbled endlessly on a pad of paper while the other made conversation with me about our well-being. At last the man with the writing pad was finished and he asked me to inform my mother of their visit. He concluded by saying that we would receive in the mail a letter of itemized articles with which the church will assist us with. And he said that we were also eligible to receive care food packages once every month. I thanked the two men and shook their hands, to which they extended well wishes to my mother and then promptly left.

I felt very elated and I wanted to run and tell my mother of these unusual visitors, and would have if I knew where she was. Someone, complete strangers, wanted to help us! They spoke of food and clothing for all of us, and maybe even beds, blankets, and pillows. Perhaps I could dress up in a beautiful dress, wear shoes made out of leather? My classmates would notice my fine clothes, gather around me, feel the leather of my shoes, and touch the material of my dress. I would be the most popular girl in my class. I would not have to wear the same dress all week which had to be washed on Sunday and worn again on Monday. I might even be able to shed my old wooden sandals with the burlap straps that weren't so old, yet were already frayed-looking. They had stretched so much that I could barely keep them on my feet.

I was so very excited at this happy news, and wanted to share it, but I was the only one home, and nobody else knew of the happenings of that day but me. So I had to sit and wait until my mother arrived home that evening. It was already rather late, so I thought it wouldn't be much longer. And so it was that I soon heard footsteps coming into the forehall. The door opened and my mother entered the room.

"Why are you sitting in the dark?" she asked. I jumped off the window bench, but made no answer. In silence, I studied her face to determine whether the news I would bring her would fill her face with pleasure and a bright smile. She had a contented expression on her face,

219

and her eyes shone with satisfaction as she announced that today she had landed a job! She was going to work for a lady who resided in the Western sector of Berlin, cleaning her house twice a week, and each time she would earn four West Marks.

"Do you realize, Rita, how much money four West Marks are when I exchange them for East Marks?" she asked triumphantly. "The exchange rate is one West Mark for seven East Marks. That means that I will have 56 Marks each week. With that money, I can buy additional bread. And there is a black market not far from the house in which I will work. I've passed it many times. People buy, sell and trade everything you can think of there, and a loaf of bread sells on the black market for 80 East Marks or 11 West marks." With her face flushed with excitement, she went on.

'Tomorrow I begin to earn my first four West Marks and in three days from now I will earn four more. The lady, Frau Neumann is an invalid. She suffered leg injuries in an air raid when she was pinned underneath a steel beam. She isn't a miserable person, though, and she is happy to be alive. Although she suffered the loss of her mother and her two daughters, also taken from her on that horrible night, she believes that God has spared her for a purpose."

In the pause following this description of mother's new employer, and unable to contain myself listening to any more of this tragedy, I pounced enthusiastically into her story to tell her about what happened to me that day. She listened in silence, with a gleam in her eyes. When I had ended my report, she took me by the shoulders and led me into a waltz rhythm, singing, "Today is our lucky day, today is our lucky day!"

Just three weeks later a letter arrived in the mail, giving the address of a storehouse where we would be able to pick up such splendor as a china cabinet, a round oak table with four chairs, an oval red coconut fiber rug, three beds complete with mattresses and blankets, clothing for all of us, including a calico rabbit fur coat for my mother, and a care package of food. These items would have to be picked up in the American sector of Berlin and hauled to our apartment by ourselves.

All the packaged items had been flown in by the organization "We Care" of the United States during the trying time known as the Berlin Blockade. Suddenly, West Berlin was cut off from food and other supplies. For 328 days from June 1948 until May 1949, the Soviets blockaded all road, rail and canal traffic from the West Zone of German to West Berlin. Their aim was to force the western powers to allow the Soviet zone to start supplying Berlin with food, fuel, and aid, thereby giving the Soviets practical control over the entire city.

In response, the Western Allies organized the Berlin Airlift to carry supplies to the people in West Berlin. Aircrews from the United States Air Force, the British Royal Air Force, the Royal Australian Air Force, the Royal New Zealand Air Force, and the South African Air Force flew over 200,000 flights in one year, providing up to 6,729 tons of necessities daily, such as fuel and food, to the Berliners.

Our family was not directly affected by the Berlin Blockade or the Airlift (although there had been some supplies that formerly came to East Berlin via West Berlin, and this was now ended). But we were affected indirectly. We could hear the constant droning of aircraft coming and going at all hours of the day and night, and the Communists were also constantly trying to belittle the effort through propaganda – trying to convince everyone on both sides of the line that the airlift would fail, and thus reduce morale in the people of West Berlin.

The starving people of West Berlin lined the airport landing strip fences by the thousands, cheering the arriving cargo planes with tears in their eyes. Once the airlift got into its full stride, one cargo aircraft was landing every 90

221

seconds, literally 24 hours per day.

Since there weren't enough military personnel to unload the planes, German men and women worked to unload these precious gifts of life in around-the-clock shifts. The process had to be worked very quickly to make room for the next plane to land. In the end, the people of West Berlin could not be starved into submission to render the whole city to the Communists.

By the spring of 1949 the effort was clearly succeeding, and by April the airlift was delivering more cargo than had previously been transported into the city by rail alone. The success of the Berlin Airlift brought embarrassment to the Soviets who had refused to believe it could make a difference. In an effort to demonstrate that their efforts to this point had not been at all a strain, on Easter Sunday of 1949 a special effort was made for a maximum effort. In one 24 hour period, over 12,000 tons of coal were delivered to West Berlin. But this was not all. As a result of the efficiencies put into place for this, what was called the "Easter Parade," the daily normal airlift capacity increased to well over 8,000 tons per day, and a hefty surplus of supplies had begun to accumulate.

On May 12, 1949, having realized that their plan to make the Western allies give up their position had failed. They announced that the blockade would be lifted. Once more the people of West Berlin went wild. As the Soviet barricades lifted, they shouted, "We are still alive, we are still alive." They hugged strangers and danced in the streets.

The efforts of the Western Allies had done what was once thought to be impossible, and had not been in vain. It was a victory not won without cost, however. There were 70 aircrew members who lost their lives in the airlift. Their names are inscribed in the Berlin Airlift Memorial which is located at the Berlin Tempelhof Airport. This will be a constant reminder for the forthcoming generations and an everlasting thanks to the Western powers.

After the blockade was lifted, the organization "We Care" continued to fly into Germany with food packages and items which were desperately needed by the 5 1/2 million people expelled by the Poles from Eastern Germany and the sick and starved prisoners of war which arrived home after years of hard labor from Siberia and the Ural.

Our family came under the category of both, and "We Care" was very even-handed – it didn't matter whether you were on the west or the east side of the line between the two Berlins.

Berlin had become the central station of desperation and confusion. War prisoners without family or quarters could be assigned to find food and shelter at a homecoming camp, also provided by the "We Care" organization. The Red Cross Search Program assisted every person to locate next of kin. I did not realize then how fortunate we were to be assigned a room of our own, for it took years just to clear away the rubble before housing could begin to be rebuilt.

It was a true marvel when the day came for our new furniture and clothing to arrive. Choruses of "Oohs" and "Aahs" broke loose when my mother and her friends began bringing in our treasures, which now made our dreary room into a warm, inviting home. The red cocoa rug was rolled out in the middle of the room and the oval oak table placed in the middle with four chairs looked just about formal compared to our previous nothing. The grey painted china cabinet fit perfectly in one corner. My mother's bed with mahogany wooden headboard was placed along the opposite wall. And there were other boxes containing blankets, clothing of appropriate sizes, and dishes. At last, there was an oval table cloth in red and black brocade with silky fringes – it was just perfect for the table.

Now our room had an aura of comfort and warmth, and I could not envision that anything could be better than it was now. Next, my mother unpacked the Care package which contained dried milk, eggs, potatoes, and dried sweet potatoes, as well as lard and flour. Out of happy exhaustion, my mother sat down on her new bed and folded her hands in her lap.

"Today," she said, "we will celebrate!"

We would celebrate my return home and that she now had all four children by her side. Her voice trembled, tears ran down her cheeks, she choked and whispered that she wished our father could be with us now. God only knew his fate. Maybe he would still return. Many prisoners are still coming home, he might be among them. After she wiped her tears with her hands, there was silence.

Abruptly, she shook her head no. She raised her voice in anger, "He is dead! He never even made it to Russia. He could not have borne the emotional strain. He knew at his last encounter with you children that you would be alone. He loved you. He could not tolerate the burden forced upon him." Her voice quieted again. "He died," she said softly, "He just died."

I felt my heart pain when the picture of him appeared unbidden in my mind. It was the picture of our last encounter with him, my father working overseen by Russian guards carrying rifles with fixed bayonets, and submachine guns, his clothes ragged and his face sad and blue with cold. The last words we heard from him as he looked sadly into our faces were, "Someday we will be together again." He did not beg the guards to release him. He tried hard to keep his composure. He knew his life was not his own any longer but belonged to the Russians forever.

Epilog

Those three months in the East Berlin jail were dreary and uncomfortable, but if they expected that the sentence would cow me and make me remain in this pit of a place, well, they were wrong. When the weeks were finally expired, as part of the process of releasing me the authorities gave me a final lecture about obeying the law, and made it very clear that I was forbidden to enter West Berlin. I was not to join my husband, and as far as they were concerned our marriage was annulled. And so at last I walked out through the gate.

My sister had engaged the services of a taxi and she and it were waiting as I emerged back into the free air. Or rather, it was as free as the air in Communist East Berlin could get, which was not very much. Yes, my enemy East Berlin wanted me to stay in its cold, clammy clutches, but I was going to break its laws one last time anyway.

It took less than an hour for me to be delivered to one of the checkpoints leading into the US Zone, and a few minutes later I was free! Really free this time. The US Consulate had my immigration paperwork all ready and in a very short time I was in the United States.

Ironically, the warning by my Communist jailers that my American husband would abandon me not long after we were together in the United States had a little of the ring of truth in it. The marriage had started out in hope, but by the time he was ready to be discharged from the Army and sent home we were already at loggerheads over one thing or another. In fact, he had indicated to me that he really didn't want me to come to the USA, after all. Of course I ignored this.

Later, as a legal resident and then citizen of the United States of America, I found the true love of my life, Donald Kyle. Our marriage lasted all the rest of his life, producing four children. In him I found a man who reminded me of my dear father: kind to his children, a good father and husband. I feel that God gave him to me to heal the pain of losing my dear father. Don passed on to the other side before me, but I will love him until my own end, and hope that I will see him again there when my time comes. I still think of them both daily and miss them.

My mother's experiences from the time my parents left to report to the Soviet Commandant on February 13, 1945, until I finally got her to tell me the whole story on March 16, 1978, were largely unknown to me. I knew some parts of the story, but until I sat down with her and a tape recorder, I had never heard the full story. The scenes of suffering and death she described exceeded anything my imagination had conceived to that point. My own experiences in the bombed out city of Prussian Holland, and the scenes of death and destruction I had viewed were now exceeded by hers.

It would be appropriate to tell her story here, but space does not permit. So it appears separately, in a volume with the title "The Bones of My People", by Gertrud Baltutt[18]. The title refers to her memory of the mass graves that were prepared for her fellow German forced

---

[18] "The Bones of My People" is available from Prospect Avenue Books.

laborers as they died in horrible, miserable conditions in the Soviet labor camps in the Ural Mountains.

Mother lived to the ripe old age of 91, and passed away in the city of Ulm-Donau, Germany, in 2004, tended at the end by her daughter Irmgard.

As for my sisters, like me, they all ended up leaving East Berlin before the infamous Berlin Wall was constructed. Irmgard married a German man originally from Leipzig and lives now in Germany near her three children and several grandchildren. The others, like me, married American soldiers and live now in the United States.

Edith lives in Colorado, and had three children and now likewise several grandchildren. Waltraut lives in Washington state. She exceeded the rest of us in number of children, with ten, and now has twelve grandchildren.

If I could only see my homeland where I was born and lived with my entire family once more, my restless soul could be content. I would walk up to the Sand Hills and let the breeze cool my face. I would then go to the very place as a child that I had called my own and would reconstruct my castle and gather all the wild flowers I once loved and again press a bouquet into the moist sand table. I would sit under the same old tree to daydream once more, and then pray to the immortal soul of my father and tell him that I am home.

I'd then walk down to the Sand Hills over to the Horse River. I don't think I would swim but I would look across the water as far as my eyes can see and remember the day when my father tossed me into the water and told me to just swim. I remember the sky as it looked then, blue and decorated with pure white scattered clouds and the water, as I ran my little hand over it, warm and crystal clear.

The pain of losing him still burns in my soul and the years have not completely healed my wounds. Looking back on yesterday, I am still his little child and in my memory he never grew old. His face remains as youthful and as handsome as the time I saw him through my child's eyes. If I could see him again, I would tell him how we struggled and how I suffered in losing my mother and him. Again I'd ask him to please forgive me and that as he said, "Someday we will be together again," we will walk together in Paradise, where there is Time no longer.

There's more to the story!

During the three and half years the Baltutt children spent, first as wolf children, and then in Berlin as orphans, their mother Gertrud was enduring a very strenuous and dangerous time as a forced laborer in the Soviet Union, specifically in the Ural Mountains.

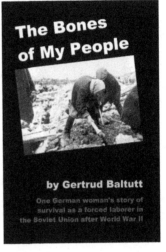

Her experience, which was shared by over 500,000 other Germans from the eastern territories of Germany (of which roughly half did not survive to return home), is told in *The Bones of My People*. This book is available from Prospect Avenue Books.

For more information about this book please visit:

www.prospectavenuebooks.com

Made in the USA
Middletown, DE
10 July 2020